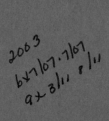

How to Design, Implement, and Interpret an Employee Survey

How to Design, Implement, and Interpret an Employee Survey

John H. McConnell

AMACOM

American Management Association

New York • Atlanta • Brussels • Buenos Aires • Chicago • London • Mexico City
San Francisco • Shanghai • Tokyo • Toronto • Washington, D.C.

This publication is designed to provide accurate and authoritative information in regard to the subject matter covered. It is sold with the understanding that the publisher is not engaged in rendering legal, accounting, or other professional service. If legal advice or other expert assistance is required, the services of a competent professional person should be sought.

Although this publication is subject to copyright, permission is granted free of charge to use and print pages from the enclosed CD-ROM. Only the original purchaser may make copies. Under no circumstances is permission granted to sell or distribute on a commercial basis material reproduced from this publication.

Library of Congress Cataloging-in-Publication Data

McConnell, John H.
   How to design, implement, and interpret an employee survey / John H. McConnell.
       p. cm.
Includes bibliographical references and index.
  ISBN 0-8144-0709-9
  1. Employee attitude surveys. I. Title.

  HF5549.5.A83 M386 2003
  658.3'14'0723—dc21

                                                          2002153914

Printing number

10 9 8 7 6 5 4 3 2 1

To Ferdinand J. Setaro:
one half of a critical partnership

CONTENTS

LIST OF FIGURES

ACKNOWLEDGMENTS

Our management consulting company has been designing, conducting, and interpreting employee opinion surveys for over twenty-five years. We initially added them to our repertoire of services because we could not find existing ones that provided the type of information our clients and we felt was required.

Since we could not locate existing surveys that met our criteria, we developed our own and are today quite proud of their results and success. However, it was not an easy task. The very first employee opinion survey we conducted was a complete disaster, and I need to acknowledge Russell Glicksman, Tom Berry, and Ferdinand Setaro, at that time human resources executives with the company that participated in that first test run. They stood by us through the painful development process, and the final product may never have been produced without them.

Robert A. Nowaczyk, an experienced user of employee opinion surveys, also contributed valuable insights over the years for their effective use.

I think every company for which we have conducted an employee opinion survey has taught us something and contributed to the development and improvement of the process. There are too many of these clients to mention here, but to each of them a thank-you.

Also to be acknowledged are Rob Kaplan, friend and agent, who contributed his knowledgeable insights; Ruth Long who made my manuscript sentences grammatically correct and my words properly spelled; Adrienne Hickey, AMACOM executive editor, who as with previous projects provided guidance and support; and Mike Sivilli, AMACOM associate editor, who produced a reader-friendlier version of the book.

To all, thank you. As must be said in every book I have written, "Thank you. I could not have done it without you."

John H. McConnell

INTRODUCTION

What we have here is a failure to communicate.

CAPTAIN (STROTHER MARTIN),
Cool Hand Luke

We seem to be a society that enjoys surveys and polls—both by participating in them and reviewing the results. We want our opinions to be known, and we want to discover how our opinions compare with those of others. The government and political parties constantly conduct polls and publish their results to support their decisions and positions. Newspapers routinely ask questions of the public regarding current events. Television programs seem to increasingly include both telephone numbers and Web site addresses for viewers to express their opinions—opinions that are often compiled and reported on during the programs. Market researchers regularly survey the public to determine its preference for products and services, and magazines offer self-analysis questionnaires on subjects ranging from financial planning to spousal relationships.

This predisposal toward using surveys is reflected in my personal experience. In just one week, the results of four polls were published in my local newspaper; five television programs I watched included call-in responses; government administrators referred to the results of three polls; a Sunday magazine offered a survey of travel habits; and I was stopped in a shopping mall and asked questions about my fast-food preferences.

One-Way Communication

All of these types of polls and surveys are primarily one-way communication vehicles. The people and organizations who conduct them do so to obtain information they have identified as somehow needed to meet their objectives. They want to discover how people react to events, decisions, and products, and they probably use the resulting responses to arrive at their decisions.

However, information from such one-way communication vehicles can sometimes lead to faulty conclusions and decisions. The Coca-Cola situation of 1985 is one example that has become a part of business folklore.

Coca-Cola Taste Tests

In the early 1980s, Coca-Cola was experiencing a serious market share challenge from Pepsi-Cola. Many people switched to diet soft drinks (Diet Coke was introduced in 1982), so the market for regular soft drinks decreased. In a number of taste tests, people indicated a preference for the taste of Pepsi-Cola and diet cola over Coca-Cola. Actually, many felt the taste of Diet Coke was closer to Pepsi-Cola's taste than to Coca-Cola's. In any event, a suggestion was made that a revision to the original Coca-Cola taste might help.

Coca-Cola experimented with what they thought might be an improved taste formula for its main product and then conducted a market research study to compare the new formula Coca-Cola with the traditional Coca-Cola flavor. The study's results indicated that people preferred the taste of the new version, so the company decided to replace the old with the new.

A major advertising campaign was designed, and the new Coca-Cola was introduced on April 23, 1985. The product met with public resistance even before it was available. The resistance was so great that the company had to abandon its plan for a replacement formula. On July 11, 1985, in what appeared to many to be a face-saving decision, Coca-Cola stated it would offer two Cokes—the new version and the old one (renamed Classic Coca-Cola).

In 2002, a trip to the supermarket uncovered only one version—Coca-Cola classic—(with the word *classic* now in small letters) on the shelves. When asked about New Coke, the department manager said he never heard of it. Apparently, New Coke just faded away.

On August 16, 2002, Coca-Cola announced that the new design for Coca-Cola classic bottles and cans would no longer bear the inscription, "Enjoy Coca-Cola Classic." That inscription would be replaced by just "Coca-Cola," and from the accompanying photograph, it appeared the word *classic* may be dropped entirely.

The Coca-Cola experience has not been forgotten. In July 2002, seventeen years after it occurred, it was mentioned in a major newspaper article describing a new drink from the company—Vanilla Coca-Cola.

The new versus old Coke decision was an expensive one and demonstrated the danger of basing decisions solely on one-way survey information. The taste survey was probably correct. People did prefer the new taste, but follow-up questions might have revealed that the public was unwilling to give up the current Coca-Cola. Consumers seemed to consider the replacement of the original version equal to having a part of our national identity destroyed.

On the other hand, a year ago a major amusement park conducted a survey of people visiting the park. Visitors were asked questions regarding operating hours and admission prices. The public indicated they preferred later operating hours and understood the need for an increase in admission prices. However, that survey went further than the Coca-Cola taste survey and included follow-up questions. These follow-up questions revealed that although the public understood the need for increased admission prices, they would visit the park less if the prices were raised.

Employee Opinion Surveys

Given the multitude of surveys to which we are exposed, it is not surprising that employers use surveys as a method to discover what employees think about their jobs, companies, and futures. If designed correctly and administered professionally, employee opinion surveys provide companies with accurate and useful information, but like many other polls and surveys, these are sometimes only one-way communication vehicles. The surveys collect the information the employer wants but do not provide feedback and follow-up to the employees.

It is the position of this book that employee opinion surveys are best used when they obtain more than just information. They are most effective when they are part of a process for effective two-way communication between the employer and the employees.

In an ideal world, such surveys would probably not be necessary. In an ideal world, there would be a free and open flow of information between employees and their employers, but, unfortunately, that is rarely the case. We do not live and work in such a world, and there are many conditions that can become roadblocks to communication within an organization.

Two-Way Employer/Employee Communication

My first job out of high school was for a small, family-owned retail store. Every Friday, after the store closed, five of us (the owner, his wife, and three employees) would go next door to a small restaurant. There, around a corner table, we would talk about the week's results. We reviewed the problems and accomplishments and made plans for the next week. The owners would describe the week's financial results, and we employees would tell of our issues, make suggestions, and discuss concerns. It was a very effective arrangement. All of us knew everything about the business, participated in directing its future, and felt fully involved, with our thoughts and ideas appreciated. I thought (in my naiveté) that that was how all businesses operated.

Subsequent jobs proved my initial experience to be far from the norm. I've discovered that more often there seems to be little understanding and communication between employees and management. Each appears to operate from its own set of motivations and perceptions and often projects those assumptions on to the other.

Assuming Two-Way Communication Is Typical

When I was a human resources executive with a manufacturing company, I participated in a half day meeting with the senior executives of the company, the company's attorney, and the pension plan actuary. The purpose of the meeting was to increase the benefits of the executive retirement program. I was relatively new with the company, and in preparing for the meeting I brought along information regarding what I believed to be the retirement needs of all our employees.

At the conclusion of the executive retirement plan discussion, I suggested we take the time remaining to review our employee retirement needs. I can still recall the reaction of the group, "Why would they want a retirement plan?" (That company, nonunion at the time, was later unionized. During the organizational campaign, the major promise made by the union was to establish a pension plan.)

Another company, an East Coast utility, held a series of management meetings over six months. The purpose was to determine whether to move its location and, if so, to where. The management found this to be a difficult problem, and it took the full six months for them to accept the need to move and select a location.

Management then called an employee meeting and announced the decision to move. The move was to be in one month. This was the first time the employees had heard of even a possible move. They were surprised and asked many questions.

The management, who took six months to accept the problem and develop a solution, could not understand why the employees could not immediately accept the decision.

Not all companies are that oblivious or uncaring of their employees' needs and perceptions. Many recognize the benefits of knowing employees' opinions of employment conditions, and employee opinion surveys have become a major device for learning what their employees want and think.

Two-Way Communication

When the employee opinion surveys are an element of an ongoing two-way communication process, they can make a significant contribution to all aspects of employee relations. This means that employees receive feedback on the survey results; the survey is followed up to better understand responses; survey results are compared with previous surveys and reported by appropriate organization groupings; the survey is used as a basis for supervisor/employee communication improvement; and results are analyzed both for employee satisfaction and importance.

Employee Opinion Survey Approaches

Over the years, a number of approaches have been developed for employee opinion surveys, and they have been assigned a variety of names. In addition to employee opinion surveys, they are called employee attitude surveys, annual employee questionnaires, morale indexes, work attitude questions, work satisfaction surveys, and company scorecards.

This book does not attempt to review every possible approach, and it does not present an academic process. It describes in detail a practical approach we developed that is used by many companies. It provides you with a method to discover what your employees' perceptions are and how to use that information to improve communication, conditions of employment, morale, and performance. In the process, it describes some of the things for which employee surveys should not be used and the consequences of so using them.

When you have completed this book, you will have all of the information required to develop, implement, and interpret an employee opinion survey as a two-way communication tool within your company. In addition, the book provides you with the flexibility necessary to allow you to customize the approach to the specific needs of your company, and the ability to use only portions of the process.

This book takes a four-step approach to developing and conducting an employee opinion survey. These steps and their chapter titles describe this approach.

Step 1. Assessing your employee opinion survey needs

❑ An overview of employee opinion surveys
❑ Start-up considerations and guidelines
❑ Identifying survey objectives
❑ Defining survey planning elements
❑ Selecting conditions of employment to survey
❑ Developing employee survey demographics

Step 2. Developing your employee opinion survey

❑ Designing survey questions
❑ Creating the survey instrument
❑ A sample employee opinion survey

Step 3. Conducting your employee opinion survey

❑ Administering the survey
❑ Tabulating and compiling survey results
❑ Considering external services and products

Step 4. Reporting your employee opinion survey results

❑ Writing and delivering reports
❑ Sample management summary reports
❑ Sample reports for employees
❑ Using your employee opinion survey for two-way communication
❑ Survey checklists

The survey implementation checklists chapter (Chapter 17) provides checklists for each of the major steps in creating and implementing your own employee opinion survey. Those checklists provide a convenient way to review each of the steps.

Most of the chapters include forms that will assist you in designing and conducting your own employee opinion survey. Those forms are also provided on an accompanying CD-ROM for you to reproduce as is or revise to meet your requirements.

Examples of good and poor use of employee opinion surveys are also a part of each chapter. These examples are all real-world situations, but in some cases, the names have been changed to protect the guilty.

So, let's begin.

PART ONE

ASSESSING YOUR EMPLOYEE OPINION SURVEY NEEDS

1

AN OVERVIEW OF EMPLOYEE OPINION SURVEYS

The first key to wisdom is this—constant and frequent questioning, for by doubting we are led to questions and by questioning to truth.

PIERRE ABELARD,
Sic et Nom

Good management is always wondering what its company's employees truly think about their jobs and the company. Management also assumes employees possess a great deal of information that can improve working conditions and operations. The method commonly used to discover what employees perceive and know is the employee opinion survey.

Management's primary objective for a survey is usually:

> To discover employee perceptions regarding satisfaction with conditions of employment.

However, some employee opinion surveys are conducted for more limited reasons and have objectives that are also more limited. For example, a survey to determine employee opinions regarding only scheduled working hours or employee benefits will limit its objectives to that single condition of employment. Such limited surveys are often considerably shorter and require less time to complete.

The procedure described in this book can be used for such limited objective surveys, but generally it is for a broader survey—one that is concerned with most, if not all, conditions of employment. *Conditions of employment* is a term that is used throughout this book. It refers to all aspects of a company that relate to individual employees.

Employee Opinion Survey Formats

To accomplish their objectives, employee opinion surveys use a variety of formats. The most typical surveys take the form of a written questionnaire, or they are conducted online, in focus groups, and in interviews. Sometimes, a company may elect to use a combination of two or more of these formats. In fact, the procedure described in this book suggests a combination of formats. Whatever the format selected, it should be the one that best meets the specific requirements of a company.

Written Employee Opinion Surveys

The written employee opinion survey format is the one most used. It consists of written questions requiring written responses. Sometimes, responses are fill-ins such as:

What one word best describes our company?

_____

Essay type questions request responses to be in full sentence format. For example:

What are the three best conditions of employment at our company and the reasons you feel make them the best?

Some written questionnaires use objective response questions, such as:

Do you prefer our company's flexible work hours policy over the previous standard work hours?

Yes _____　　No _____

Other written questionnaires utilize multiple-choice response questions. For example:

How satisfied are you with the employees' parking assignments?

Very satisfied　　　　　　　　　　　　_____
Somewhat satisfied　　　　　　　　　　_____
Neither satisfied nor dissatisfied　　_____
Somewhat dissatisfied　　　　　　　　_____
Very dissatisfied　　　　　　　　　　　_____

Some written surveys are in a consumable format; that is, the survey participants record their responses directly on the written survey. Each survey questionnaire may then be used only with a single participant. At other times, the survey questionnaire and the answer sheets are separate documents.

For example, a small booklet may contain the questions, and the participant's responses are recorded on an answer sheet provided with the booklet. This approach allows the question booklets to be reused, and the individual answer sheets are generally easier to tabulate.

Later chapters will deal with all of these types of written response questions and how to use them.

Written Employee Opinion Survey Administration

Written employee opinion surveys can be administered in several ways. Some companies mail the surveys to the participants at their homes or work locations with a request to complete and return the survey by mail. Some companies administer written surveys to groups of employees on company property. Other times, the surveys are available at specific company locations (such as the human resources department). Employees can stop and complete the surveys at these locations, or pick them up and later return the completed survey to the same location.

Each of these administrative methods has advantages and disadvantages. Which you should use depends on several factors that will be detailed later in this book.

Written Employee Opinion Survey Costs

Written surveys have traditionally been the least expensive to administer and, depending on the type of responses, to tabulate and report. However, in recent years, online employee opinion surveys have been increasingly used. Once programmed, these online surveys are often less expensive to administer and tabulate.

Online Employee Opinion Surveys

Online employee opinion surveys have many of the same advantages of a written survey. They also use the same type of questions. The only difference between online and written surveys is that the questions in an online survey are displayed on a terminal screen and responses are entered via a mouse or keyboard. The two examples below are from online surveys.

How satisfied are you with the training you received for your current job?

Very satisfied	_____
Somewhat satisfied	_____
Neither satisfied nor dissatisfied	_____
Somewhat dissatisfied	_____
Very dissatisfied	_____

Have you used the company's employee hotline during the last year?

Yes _____   No _____

Usually, one question at a time is displayed on the screen along with the method for response. Some online surveys allow the participant to go back to previous questions. Others only allow the participant to move forward through the survey questions.

Online Employee Opinion Survey Administration

Online employee opinion surveys by their very design require individual administration. It is rare that they are administered to groups of employees in the same room at the same time.

In some companies, computers to be used for the survey are located in specific areas and employees participate according to their schedules. In a company at which most employees have computers, the survey can be made available directly to each employee through his computer. Some companies have even made the survey available to employees at their home computers via the Internet.

Online Employee Opinion Survey Costs

The major advantage an online employee opinion survey has over a written survey is its ability to immediately tabulate and combine responses. Then, by creating a database of responses, the results can be reported by numerous employee groupings, making interpretation more flexible. This allows for faster and more comprehensive analysis of survey results at a lower cost.

Though there are expenses to program the initial survey, later and similar surveys generally require little reprogramming, so this is a very cost-effective method to gather data.

Focus Group Employee Opinion Surveys

Focus group employee opinion surveys are conducted with small numbers of employees—usually six to twelve. They are conducted conference style by trained facilitators who provide discussion procedure but no content, so only the participants' thoughts and opinions are collected. Sometimes, the groups include completion of written surveys along with discussion.

Focus Group Employee Opinion Survey Administration

A focus group begins with exercises to put the participants at ease and to explain the group objective and method of operation. Then predetermined areas and questions are presented in a manner designed to produce discussion and obtain the group's overall perceptions and individual reasoning.

For example, a focus group might begin with the participants individually ranking several conditions of employment based on their satisfaction with each condition. Next, an exercise to combine the individual rankings into a group ranking reveals the basis for their degrees of satisfaction.

In another group approach, the participants are requested to describe the three best features and three poorest features of several conditions of employment. Again, the reasoning behind each participant's answer as well as the group's collective perception is gathered by the facilitator.

The ability to identify the basis for employee opinions is the main advantage of this approach. Its main disadvantage is, due to the small number of employees that can be included in any one group, it is difficult to conduct focus groups with all employees. Since the time and cost may be too great, this survey is most used when there is a relatively small employee population to canvass, or when it is conducted with a random sample of employees rather than the entire population.

Sometimes, this survey is used in concert with written and online employee opinion surveys. For example, after a written or online survey is administered and tabulated, areas requiring additional information can be used as the basis for focus groups.

Focus Group Employee Opinion Survey Costs

Since only a few employees can participate in each focus group, each meeting is usually one to two hours in length, and a skilled facilitator is required. This survey is usually more expensive to conduct than written and online surveys.

Employee Opinion Survey Interviews

Interviews offer the same advantages as focus groups for obtaining reasons behind opinions, and they are capable of providing even more specificity. A skilled interviewer can explore in depth a participant's perceptions in any given area, but interviews are even more costly and time-consuming to conduct with large groups of employees.

Employee Opinion Survey Interview Administration

Employee opinion survey interviews use predetermined questions. Often, they use the same questions that are used in a written or an online survey. The difference is that follow-up questions can also be used. For example, the interviewer can ask:

How satisfied are you with the company's health insurance?

The interviewer may then provide a selection of responses:

Very satisfied _____
Somewhat satisfied _____
Neither satisfied nor dissatisfied _____
Somewhat dissatisfied _____
Very dissatisfied _____

Once answered, the interviewer can then ask:

What are the three best and three poorest aspects of the health insurance?

The interviewer can continue to probe deeper with questions.

Employee opinion survey interviews generally take thirty minutes to an hour and must be conducted by a skilled interviewer. Interviews are one-on-one situations, so they limit the number of employees that can participate in a survey at any one time and increase the cost of administration.

Like focus groups, this format is often used for random samplings and/or follow-ups to a written or online employee opinion survey.

However, for political reasons, some organizations use this method with their senior executives (more on this later).

Employee Opinion Survey Interview Costs

The same factors that make focus group surveys more costly than written and online surveys apply to interview surveys but even more so. They usually become cost-effective only when there is a very small employee population, so generally they are conducted with random samples of employees, as follow-ups, or with a specific group.

Which Format Should You Use?

Which survey format you use depends on several factors you should consider:

> What are the reasons for which you are conducting the survey?
>
> How many employees do you have to survey?
>
> How much time will your survey require to complete?
>
> Which format best fits the culture of your company and abilities of your employees?
>
> What is the employee survey history at your company?

What Are the Reasons for Conducting the Survey?

The basic objective of most employee opinion surveys is to obtain information, but to determine a survey format, you need to consider for what reason or reasons you want the information. Those reasons will govern the design of the survey questions and responses and determine which employees will be asked to participate.

Chapter 2 will help you to identify and evaluate your reasons, but at this point, it is important to recognize that the survey's purpose will determine how many employees to survey, how many locations to survey, how many questions to ask, what types of questions to ask, and in how many ways the results must be reported.

How Many Employees Do You Have to Survey?

As discussed, written and online surveys lend themselves for use with large employee populations. A typical survey in both of these formats usually requires an hour to complete and can be administered individually or in scheduled groups. These formats also are effective when employees are scattered at a number of locations.

If your employee population is small, you can consider focus groups and interviews. If you feel that one of these approaches is needed and you have a large employee population, you can consider conducting interviews or focus groups with a random sampling of employees or as a follow-up to a written or online employee opinion survey.

Random Sampling

Random sampling is a selection of some employees who will represent the entire employee population from which they are drawn. This could mean selecting employees to represent all your employees or subgroups.

The key to successful random sampling is to ensure it is random. If not, the results of the survey will be skewed to the bias of the group. In such a case, the survey results will not be reliable for all employees.

A later chapter will review how to select a random sample.

How Much Time Will Your Survey Require to Complete?

There are three time considerations:

The length of time required to complete an individual survey

The date by which the entire survey is to be completed

The time frame for conducting the survey

The Length of Time Required to Complete an Individual Survey

Earlier, it was suggested that written and online surveys generally require one hour each to complete, focus groups an hour to two hours with six to twelve participants, and interviews thirty minutes to an hour to complete. Specific surveys may require different times, depending on the number of areas to be surveyed and their design. Once you have selected the format to use and can estimate the time for each survey, you can calculate the total time required to achieve your task.

Actually, calculating time requirements may cause you to revise your format selection. For example, you may have been considering focus groups for your survey, but on determining the total time they would require, decide to use a written survey format. On the other hand, you may have been planning to use an online survey, but after discovering the time required, decide you could add a few focus groups.

The Date by Which the Entire Survey Is to Be Completed

Once you know the time required for the surveys, you need to consider when they must be completed. The question to answer is: Do you have enough time to complete the surveys using the selected format?

For example, if you are considering a one-hour online survey but only have a few computers for employees to use, scheduling may not allow you to complete the survey by its due date. You may have to consider a different format or random sampling.

You also have to factor whether employees are going to participate during or outside of their normal working hours. If the survey is to be completed during normal working hours, you need to consider how long you can have employees away from their jobs, how many employees can be away from their jobs and/or departments at one time, and if overtime pay is required (if the survey is to be completed outside usual working hours).

The Time Frame for Conducting the Survey

Finally, you must consider the time frame in which you want the survey completed. This refers to the length of time between the first survey and the last. When all employees take the survey at relatively the same time, there is a greater degree of consistency in response, but as the time frame is increased, other factors may affect results. Employees who have already taken the survey may discuss it with others. In addition, other occurrences may impact employee perceptions. For example, when the first survey is conducted, company orders may be substantial but could decrease (over a long period) by the final surveys. Such a condition could cause a change in employees' perceptions of their security.

Which Format Best Fits the Culture of Your Company and the Skills of Your Employees?

If your employees have some computer literacy and computer accessibility, online surveys may make sense, but if they do not possess these skills, you want to avoid the online format. Attempting to administer an online survey can be counterproductive when employees are unfamiliar with computers. They make mistakes, and in some cases do not participate. The situation in Florida during the 2000 presidential election is an example of the types of problems that can be created when your survey population is forced to respond using unfamiliar techniques.

If your employees or any portion of them cannot read or cannot read English, you have to design your format accordingly. For example, you can use answer sheets and have someone read the questions and alternative responses to groups of employees.

A small manufacturing facility in Maine conducted a written employee opinion survey of its production workers. Unbeknownst to the company, a number of employees were illiterate. These employees were embarrassed, so to hide their deficiency, they merely placed random marks on the answer sheets.

The company, still not knowing the problem, accepted the results and made several decisions that impacted employee benefits. Unfortunately, the decisions created major employee relations problems since the company did not respond to actual employee opinions.

Every company has a culture with which employees are familiar. In some companies, employee meetings are a regular occurrence, so employees are comfortable with that approach with focus groups. At other companies, a meeting may be so out of the ordinary it can make participation difficult.

Other companies may communicate with employees through e-mail. In such an organization, an individual online employee opinion survey may seem natural.

The important consideration is to select a format with which employees will be comfortable and can interact.

What Is the Employee Survey History at Your Company?

If your company has regularly conducted employee opinion surveys, always consider the previous format that was used. If you change the format, you need to describe the change, explain why the change was made, and make sure the information collected by the new format can be combined with information from the previous surveys.

A Washington State financial services company had been conducting employee opinion surveys for several years. It had always used a written survey of approximately eighty questions, and reported results by twenty-two different cuts.

In 2001, the company decided to change to a computer-based survey. All its employees were computer literate and had desktop computers. What wasn't considered were the results from previous years. In order to do all of the comparisons it wanted, the company had to have all its past survey responses entered into a database. Since there were one hundred employees and five years of surveys (each with eighty questions), the result was a total of 40,000 entries that had to be entered into a database.

These are the considerations in selecting a survey format. Others include the type of skills available to you for designing, administering, and interpreting a survey. Later chapters of this book provide more information to assist you in selecting the best format for your company's survey. At this point, it is important that you are aware of the various approaches and basic reasons for the selection of one.

Conclusion

Each company has to select the employee opinion survey format that best fits its needs, demographics, and objectives. All of the items discussed here should be considered, as well as others that have not been mentioned. Although not as common, these can include requirements produced by political situations, contractual conditions, and corporate directives. These can be very real and cannot be ignored.

In the next chapter, a recommended approach and format will be described.

CHAPTER 2

START-UP CONSIDERATIONS AND GUIDELINES

If you don't know what is wrong with … (someone), ask him. He may tell you.

G. A. KELLY (QUOTED BY D. BANNISTER AND
FAY FRANSELLA IN *INQUIRING MAN*)

The previous chapter reviewed the basic employee opinion survey formats and introduced factors to consider in determining the most appropriate format for your company. In addition to the formats described, there are many variations, and describing all of them in detail is beyond the scope of a single book.

This chapter recommends a specific format that is the basis for the remainder of the book. It is a very practical approach. It follows Kelly's guideline (quoted above) and just asks the employees what you want to know. This chapter provides important guidelines—do's and don'ts—to avoid common pitfalls and achieve successful results.

A Recommended Format

The employee opinion survey format this book recommends is a combination of elements from several of the ones described. It is:

> A written survey administered to groups of employees or an online self-administered survey

> Follow-up focus groups and/or interviews to obtain any additional required information

> A survey report that includes:

> ❑ Analysis of all conditions of employment

> ❑ Satisfaction and importance perceptions for each condition of employment

> ❑ Comparisons with past survey results

> ❑ Management reactions results for each condition of employment

> Use of survey results in two-way communication

> Development of objectives based on survey results

Development Steps

The specific development and implementation steps for this format as covered in this book are:

> Establish a specific objective for the survey.

> Identify the purposes for which survey information will be used.

> Identify the employee population to survey.

> Identify the conditions of employment and their subareas to survey.

> Determine where and when to survey.

> Determine the employee demographics to identify and report.

> Select the types of questions and responses.

Develop the questions for each area.

Sequence the questions.

Develop a security system.

Prepare the survey documents.

Prepare the survey administration rules and instructions.

Select the survey administrators.

Describe the tabulation report format.

Schedule the survey.

Notify the employees.

Train the administrators.

Obtain supplies and equipment.

Administer the survey.

Analyze the initial tabulation.

Obtain additional required information.

Prepare a final report to employees.

Deliver the final report to employees.

Prepare individual supervisor reports.

Train the supervisors in a survey report meeting method.

Conduct supervisor-led survey report meetings.

Now, before we take the first step, there are a few pitfalls of which you should be aware.

Pitfalls

The following pitfalls, if not avoided, can make your employee opinion survey less than effective and useful:

Lack of a clear objective for the survey

No management support

No communication to employees

No confidentiality protection

No credibility

Nonobjective administration

Results not delivered as promised

Attempting to affect results

Using a survey as a voting device

Each of these pitfalls has been used to create a guideline that, if followed, will avoid the negative results of the pitfall and contribute to a successful employee opinion survey.

Employee Opinion Survey Guidelines

The following guidelines are designed to avoid some of the common pitfalls of employee opinion surveys. Those pitfalls can negatively impact a survey, its results, and the use of those results. The guidelines are:

Do not conduct an employee opinion survey without a clear and specific objective.

Obtain management support for a complete survey plan before beginning development.

Be sure you have fully and timely communicated the objective of the survey and use of its results to all employees.

Make provisions to protect employee confidentiality.

Administer the survey objectively.

Deliver survey results as promised.

Do not attempt to affect survey results.

Do not use an employee opinion survey for voting.

Do Not Conduct an Employee Opinion Survey Without a Clear and Specific Objective

This guideline cannot be stressed too strongly. It seems logical not to begin a survey without an objective, yet it is not an uncommon action.

This seems to occur when the company has access to a survey format and decides to implement it without ensuring the format meets the company's needs.

As one company's human resources vice president remarked, "Many of our past surveys can best be described as ready, fire, aim."

Without an objective, a survey may obtain a great deal of unusable data or miss getting the information you need. Chapter 3 will provide you with an approach to identify a specific and clear objective for your survey along with a description of the purposes for which the obtained information will be used.

> A New Mexico–based manufacturer used the services of a human resources consultant to develop its employee procedures. The consultant suggested the company conduct an employee opinion survey. The company accepted the suggestion, and without the consultant's assistance, purchased a standard published survey, and conducted it with all employees.
>
> When the results were received, no one knew what to do with them. The company contacted the consultant who reviewed what had occurred, and determined there was little useful information obtained by the survey.

Obtain Management Support for a Complete Survey Plan Before Beginning Development

Once you have established a clear objective for a survey, be sure the management of the company supports it and the plan to accomplish it. Whatever you do, do not begin the survey process without such support, and if management will not provide it, you are probably better off not attempting the survey.

> The senior management of a Nebraska food-processing company asked the vice president of human resources to prepare an employee opinion survey. The vice president did and submitted it with an implementation plan to the senior management group. His accompanying memo requested any change by a spe-

cific date. He received none, so he implemented the survey.

When the results of the survey were communicated to the senior managers, they decided not to communicate them to employees. However, that was not what the vice president of human resources had promised when the survey was announced.

When the senior managers were told that the employees were upset about not receiving survey results as promised, they blamed it on the vice president of human resources who then resigned.

Be Sure You Have Fully and Timely Communicated the Objective of the Survey and Use of Its Results to All Employees

If you want truthful opinions from your employees, you must be truthful with your communication to them. Tell them exactly what the purpose of the survey is and how its results will be used. If you do not fully and timely communicate to them, you should not be surprised if they assume other objectives for the survey. Such assumptions can create faulty results.

A Connecticut printing company was planning an employee opinion survey. However, management kept the planning secret and only announced it a few days before it was administered.

During the time the survey was being developed, a rumor had started that the company was planning to move to Tennessee. Actually, there were no such plans, but when the survey was announced, the employees felt it was the first step in planning for the move. This perception greatly changed their responses.

Make Provisions to Protect Employee Confidentiality

Employees generally respond more openly when the survey is anonymous. That means that the employees have to believe their responses are held in confidence and not identified with specific employees.

ATexas-based petroleum company believed it had several employees who were causing problems in their departments, but it was unsure exactly who they were. A decision was made to conduct an employee opinion survey to identify them.

The company felt the survey had to be anonymous to obtain the type of negative opinions they needed to identify the problem employees, so the survey did not request names or any other identifying data. However, the survey forms were secretly coded with pin pricks under the staples. This allowed the completed surveys to be identified with specific employees.

The survey was conducted. The problem employees were identified. They were fired or transferred, but eventually the other employees learned of the deception. The employees' opinions of their company were not only reduced, the company's ability to conduct future meaningful surveys was destroyed.

Ensure the Survey Process Is Perceived as Credible

The results of an employee opinion survey require honest responses from employees. If employees feel the process is not being conducted professionally, the survey will be perceived as lacking credibility, and responses and results will not be accurate.

AMontana computer services company decided to conduct its first employee opinion survey. The human resources manager used a survey she had administered at another company, and had one of the department's high school interns administer it. However, no training was given the intern.

At the survey completion meeting, the intern was unable to answer most questions, and also revealed that he and some additional part-time employees would be tabulating results. To the employees, the entire procedure was very unprofessional, so many survey forms were submitted without answers. Others just had the same response to every question.

Administer the Survey Objectively

Confidentiality also applies to the administration of the survey and how employees perceive that administration. If the survey is to be anonymous, in addition to providing individual security, the employees need to perceive that the administration is fair. This also requires ensuring that each employee can only participate one time.

A Cincinnati-based warehousing company used a written employee opinion survey that was mailed to each employee via the company mail. The surveys were delivered at about the same time.

In a number of departments, the employees met and arrived at group decisions for answering each question. They then individually used those answers to complete their individual questionnaires.

Deliver Survey Results as Promised

In addition to being truthful in communicating how survey results will be used, also deliver them as promised.

At a Louisville insurance company, management promised to report the results of the survey to all employees. Two months after the completion of the survey, a booklet was sent to all employees describing the survey, its results, and management's reactions. The responses to questions concerning performance reviews were conspicuously absent.

An employee initiated a petition demanding the results. It was signed by 85 percent of the employees and sent to the president. Management at last recognized the problem they had created and held employee meetings to explain their position.

Do Not Attempt to Affect Survey Results

Sometimes, it is tempting to take actions that will affect results—most often to improve them. That can produce an incorrect set of responses.

One year a Virginia-based manufacturing plant administered its annual employee opinion survey the week holiday bonuses were paid. It did so in an attempt to show improved employee morale to its New York-based headquarters. In addition, the plant played Christmas music in the rooms in which the survey was completed.

In this case, the behaviors were so obviously an attempt to affect results, the employees' opinions sank from the previous year.

However, you also need to recognize that unplanned events can also impact survey results.

A New York City financial company scheduled an employee opinion survey for September 14, 2001. They quickly recognized that the events of September 11, 2001, would greatly affect its outcome, so they wisely postponed.

Do Not Use an Employee Opinion Survey for Voting

Employee opinion surveys are to discover employee perceptions of conditions of employment. This does not make them ballots. When surveys are used for voting, they generally disappoint everyone.

A Michigan auto parts manufacturer was considering a change in dependant health insurance coverage. It had developed two alternatives and wanted to know which one to select. It decided to include in its annual employee opinion survey the question: Which of the two following changes to our dependant health insurance do you want to see implemented? The survey then described the two alternatives.

CHAPTER 3

IDENTIFYING SURVEY OBJECTIVES

If you don't have a plan for where you want to go, how do you know if you are lost?

JAMES L. HAYES

Management is a proactive activity. It does not wait for something to happen and then react. Instead, it decides what it wants to accomplish and then prepares plans to obtain its goal.

Employee opinion surveys are a management activity. Like all management activities, they require a plan to be successful, and the first step in planning is to identify a clear and specific objective. That objective then becomes the guideline for developing a comprehensive plan to design, conduct, and use an employee opinion survey.

In this chapter, we will examine methods for determining your survey objective and developing an implementation plan—what, who, and when to survey.

The Overall Survey Objective

To develop a comprehensive survey objective, you need to answer three questions:

1. Why do you want to conduct an employee opinion survey?
2. What are the areas in which you want to know the employees' opinions?
3. What employees do you want to survey?

These three questions are interrelated, and your answers to them will allow you to clearly establish your overall objective and describe the purposes for which the information obtained from the survey will be used.

Let's consider these three questions and your possible answers to them. Then your answers can be used to develop an objective for your survey and a plan for implementation.

Why Do You Want to Conduct an Employee Opinion Survey?

Employee opinion surveys have been conducted for a wide variety of reasons—some of which are not a good use of the process.

To indicate concern and interest for employees' opinions

To allow employees to "vote" on a specific course of action or activity

To identify problems

If other companies are doing surveys, so should we

To a certain extent, all of the above reasons can be part of an objective for conducting an employee opinion survey, but when they become the sole objective, they can create unintended problems.

To Indicate Concern and Interest for Employees' Opinions

Concern and interest by management in employees' opinions is, on the surface, an excellent management behavior, but only when it is real and not the only reason for the survey. Conducting a survey for the sole purpose of implying concern and interest is condescending at best.

A Connecticut-based heath services firm held a supervisory meeting regarding employee morale. Several supervisors mentioned their employees had expressed concern that the company seemed to have little interest in their opinions. Apparently, this resulted from a recent change in office hours. The change had been decided and announced by management without any prior communication with employees.

Following the meeting, the senior executives met and decided to conduct an employee opinion survey—although a very brief one—a single page with ten questions.

The purpose was to indicate to the employees that management was concerned about their opinions. However, the executives had little real interest in the results. In fact, the completed questionnaires were never even reviewed, let alone responses compiled and analyzed. Instead, the questionnaires were discarded.

The ruse was discovered when one of the employees saw the questionnaires in the rubbish and told other employees. So, the entire effort only further confirmed the employees' perceptions that their management had no interest in their opinions. Not surprisingly, morale further declined.

Even if the discarded surveys had not been discovered, it would have soon been apparent that the employees' opinions had no impact on management's actions.

To Allow Employees to "Vote" on a Specific Course of Action or Activity

One of the guidelines introduced in Chapter 2 was not to use surveys for voting. It described the problems that can occur in attempting to implement voting results, which is an abdication of management's responsibility.

Since we live in a democracy, voting may seem like a good approach, but sometimes it is inappropriate. A better approach might be to identify employee needs and then design and introduce a change to meet those needs.

There is also another consideration to take into account when you have employees vote on working conditions. In doing so, the company is in effect requesting concerted action, or as one labor attorney commented:

> Such a company is recognizing the employees as an organized group for determining working conditions—a de facto union. Such a company might find itself unionized without ever having an election. On the other hand, in an already unionized environment, such an approach might be objected to by the union as a company attempt to bypass the union and deal directly with employees on such matters.

All this is not to imply that seeking employee opinions regarding such situations should be avoided. Employee opinion surveys can provide an excellent way to determine what is most acceptable. The problems occur when they become votes. The same information can be gathered without making it a vote.

To Identify Problems

One purpose of employee opinion surveys is to identify problems or potential problem areas, but when that is the sole objective for the survey, it may produce unintended consequences.

> A South Dakota bank conducted an employee opinion survey to identify any departments in which employees were currently dissatisfied with company policies. The survey accomplished that, and the bank began to make plans to correct some of the situations reported. However, they ignored all survey information that was not specifically problem-related.
>
> Had the company taken the time to analyze all results from the survey, they would have discovered a number of issues that were not currently problems, but that had the potential for becoming serious concerns. However, that was outside its objective, so those areas were overlooked.

If Other Companies Are Doing Surveys, So Should We

In the 1970s, many computer salespeople discovered companies who were motivated to purchase a computer or upgrade their current computers when told their competitors had just done so. The decisions seemed to be made not to meet an identified need, but because the salespeople did not want their competitors to be one up on them.

A Baltimore-based carpet manufacturer was concerned it was losing sales to a competitive firm. At a recent industry trade conference, the competitor had used a demonstration of stain resistance that most customers found ridiculous. However, the Baltimore firm decided the competitor must know something and the demonstration must be good since it was gaining market share.

With this thought in mind, it canceled a well-planned approach and instead initiated its own version of the same stain-resistance demonstration. Needless to say, it was ineffective.

The point is that whatever management does, it should be to meet the identified needs of your company. Other companies have their own needs, and copying them will only assist you by accident.

A Good Objective

Okay, so what's a good survey objective? A good objective for an employee opinion survey is one that is based on a specific reason for the survey, including the purposes for the information. In most cases, the earlier example of an overall survey objective probably describes the primary goal:

> To discover employee perceptions regarding their satisfaction with the conditions of employment.

If you are planning a survey for a limited reason, such as just to discover opinions regarding compensation, the overall objective can be modified:

To discover employee perceptions regarding their satisfaction with the company's compensation program.

We will be using an Employee Opinion Survey Planning Form (illustrated in Figure 3-1) in this chapter to develop an objective, uses of the information, and an initial plan for your company's employee opinion survey.

The first item on the form is the overall objective. You can use the example provided or create another one that better describes your goal. Write your overall objective in one sentence beginning with the word "To."

Information Purposes

With your overall objective written, the next step (and the next item on the form) is the Information Purposes. There can be one or several purposes for information. They should describe exactly for what the information obtained from the survey will be used. Here, you want to be sure you are not limiting the use of survey information to the point it does not meet the overall objective. You may include reasons that were earlier described as not appropriate for the sole objective of the survey. For example, the purposes listed for a survey could be:

To identify areas requiring management attention

To identify changes in employee perceptions from previous surveys

To communicate to employees their collective degree of satisfaction with all conditions of employment

To discover employees' satisfaction along with their perceptions of the importance of working conditions

To form the basis of a continuing two-way communication process

To Identify Areas Requiring Management Attention

This is significantly different from identifying problem areas. Here, the concern is the early (hopefully) identification of areas that are problems or may become problems. In addition, areas of high satisfaction may provide opportunities for management to build on that satisfaction.

Figure 3-1. Employee opinion survey planning form.

Objective: To

Information Purposes

What to Survey

A small New Hampshire electronic parts manufacturer discovered through an employee opinion survey that employees were concerned that their wages were not keeping pace with those of others in the geographic area. The company immediately conducted a wage survey for its area and published the results. The wage survey indicated that the company was one of the better payers in the area. By making this correct information available in a timely fashion, the manufacturer avoided what may have been a serious morale problem.

Moreover, the company announced that it would thereafter conduct such a survey annually and publish the results.

A Nevada-based service company discovered through an employee opinion survey that its employees perceived the career development programs offered by the company to be the best in the area. The company investigated and decided they were correct. It then began to use those programs in their recruiting efforts and found they were of great assistance.

To Identify Changes in Employee Perceptions from Previous Surveys

One useful feature of annual employee opinion surveys is that, assuming questioning is similar from year to year, changes in employee perceptions can be identified.

For example, some areas traditionally receive low ratings at companies. Compensation is one such area. Perhaps it is because employees feel that being too positive about their compensation may be interpreted as not wanting an increase. Whether or not that is the reason, compensation is often rated low.

A West Virginia–based utility had the highest pay rates in the area, and this was recognized by the employees. In fact, several local newspaper articles had mentioned it. In addition, the employees were unionized, and even the union had communicated the fact in its newsletter.

> Yet, whenever a survey was conducted, the employees indicated they felt their compensation was low compared to other companies in the area.

Another area that frequently receives low ratings is communication. It seems that no matter how well a company attempts to communicate with its employees, there are always rumors. When a rumor becomes a reality, the perceptions are that full communication had not occurred.

While compensation and communication are areas that generally receive low ratings on surveys, there are other areas that receive low marks, and often they are unique to a company. That is why being able to compare results with those from previous surveys at a company is so valuable.

Over a period of time during which employee opinion surveys are regularly conducted, a company is able to identify a typical response to conditions of employment. That provides a base against which survey information can be measured and compared.

For example, if results in an area are fairly consistent from year to year, but one year is significantly different, either higher or lower than the typical, it is an area that needs to be further explored. This is a form of management by exception. It accepts there may be no "correct" evaluations, but when there are consistent ones, an exception requires attention.

To Communicate to Employees Their Collective Degree of Satisfaction with All Conditions of Employment

Asking employees to provide their perceptions may meet the company's needs, but the needs of the employees should also be recognized. If employees are surveyed and never hear anything about the results, they quickly lose interest in providing information. However, when they are surveyed, the results are communicated to them, and management reacts appropriately to the results, employees view the survey as a significant communication device.

This requires management to be as open, honest, and truthful as it desires the employees to be with survey responses. The worst thing management can do is attempt to put a spin on the results—imply they mean something they don't. This is a dangerous approach since the employees know how they responded, and it can quickly lead to a loss of faith in management.

> The employees of a Detroit nonferrous metals fabricator indicated through a survey that they were dissatisfied with the company's vacation policy. The company closed the plant for two weeks in August and required all employees to take their vacations at that time.
>
> The reason for the vacation shutdown was based on order flow. A majority of the company's major customers were closed in August, so orders were low. The company operated with a lean workforce, so it made economic and operating sense to close at that time and have a full complement of employees at all other times.
>
> However, instead of stating these reasons to the employees after the survey, the company tried to imply its policy was to allow all employees to take vacations during the most desirable time of the year. Although the employees were not aware of the real reasons for the company's policy, they recognized that the one provided was false.

The above story emphasizes another point regarding employee opinion surveys. Management does not have to change policy when employees indicate a low satisfaction in an area. It may not be possible to change, and if changes are made for every low rating, policies could be in perpetual motion. What is important is that management fully communicate with the workforce—providing honest reactions and explanations.

To Discover Employees' Satisfaction Along with Their Perceptions of the Importance of Working Conditions

Almost all employee opinion surveys seek to discover how satisfied employees are with conditions of employment. Of equal value and use are their perceptions of how important the various conditions of employment are.

For example, an employee opinion survey may discover there are two areas in which employees are dissatisfied: security and job assignments. Without knowing the importance of these areas to employees, it is difficult for a company to decide how to proceed.

If the survey also identified that security was of low importance to the employees while job assignments were of major importance, focusing company assets on both areas might prove a waste of time. Improving security may raise satisfaction, but in an area of little importance to employees. However, improving job assignments will increase satisfaction with a condition of employment that has great significance.

To Form the Basis of a Continuing Two-Way Communication Process

As stated in the Introduction, we believe this to be the most ideal purpose for conducting an employee opinion survey. It incorporates all of the favorable items already mentioned and carries them further to an integrated approach to operations.

Employee opinion surveys provide a method for employees to communicate to management and management to then respond to employees. This communication process can be maximized by using cascading meetings to discuss survey results. Supervisors can meet with their employees, examine the survey results, and take appropriate actions at the departmental level. Such an approach uses the survey information to improve working conditions and involves the supervisor and employees in a team effort.

Describing Your Purposes

You have already determined the overall objective for your survey and examined some purposes for which the survey results can be used.

Beneath the Information Purposes section of the survey planning form, record the purposes for which you will be using the information obtained from your survey. Again, write each in one sentence beginning with the word *To,* and write them in descending order of importance; that is, write the most important purpose first, the next most important purpose second, and so on until you have listed all your purposes.

If you have more than eight purposes listed, you may want to review them to determine:

Is each too detailed, limited, or specific?

Is it possible to combine two or more?

Are all really important?

You can have more than eight, but be certain all of them are really purposes for which the information is required and will be used.

Conclusion

With an objective established and the uses of the information described, you can move on to three other elements of the planning process: what, who, and when.

CHAPTER 4

DEFINING SURVEY PLANNING ELEMENTS

There's never time to do it right, but always time to do it over.

JOHN MESKIMEN,
The Wall Street Journal, March 14, 1974

Managers are proactive people. They make things happen, and good planning is the best method to ensure things happen correctly. This is particularly true with activities such as employee opinion surveys. You need to identify what you want to survey, who you want to survey, and when you want to survey.

What to Survey

Having determined why you wish to conduct a survey, the logical next step is to determine what to survey. For what areas do you want to know employees' opinions? Most often, you will be considering the various conditions of employment at your company. Other times, you may only have a single area or very limited number of areas to survey. For example, perhaps if you are interested in obtaining employee perceptions regarding a new facility, that may be the only area for which you are seeking information. In such situations, a survey is usually a one-time process.

Conditions of employment will vary by company due to the type of employment, facilities, geographic location, industry, and company size. A company that provides no benefits cannot survey opinions regarding current benefits. However, it could survey satisfaction with not having benefits. A manufacturing plant that works only one shift has no reason to survey satisfactions with shift assignments.

In our twenty-five years of conducting employee opinion surveys, the conditions of employment we have most often been requested to survey, along with their definitions, are:

- ❐ *Immediate Supervision*—the direction, planning, and control exercised by the individual to whom you report

- ❐ *Job Assignment*—the responsibilities and authorities of the job you are asked to perform

- ❐ *Communications*—the communication you receive and provide

- ❐ *Performance Measurement*—the evaluation of your individual job performance

- ❐ *Compensation*—the cash rewards you receive for your work

- ❐ *Benefits*—the noncash rewards you receive for your work

- ❐ *Security*—the confidence you have in your safety and continuation of employment

- ❐ *Executive Management*—the leadership, planning, and control exercised by the senior executives of the company

- ❐ *Equal Treatment*—the fair and nondiscriminatory treatment you and other employees receive

- ❐ *Training*—the training provided for your current job, changes to your job, and future jobs

- ❐ *Career Opportunities*—the opportunities to increase your accountability and grow within the company

- ❐ *Facilities*—the environment in which you work and the availability of necessary equipment and supplies

❐ *Overall Company*—all the things that contribute to the company and its operations

Although these are the most consistently requested conditions of employment that are surveyed:

Their definitions differ between organizations.

Not all conditions are requested by every company.

Many companies have areas not included in the list.

For the balance of this book, these conditions of employment are referred to as dimensions. Your survey does not have to include all these dimensions, and it can include others not mentioned here. It also does not have to use the above definitions. You can create your own definitions. What is important is that the dimensions to be surveyed are identified and defined in advance.

Identifying Dimensions to Survey

You may already have a list of dimensions to survey. Perhaps you have conducted surveys in the past, and you have a list of the areas questioned in those surveys. Perhaps someone or some department, such as human resources, has identified the areas to survey, or perhaps you are considering using a published survey instrument that includes predetermined dimensions.

Whatever the case, you need to determine for what dimensions you require information, so even if you have a list, you need to confirm it, the definitions, and the relationships of the dimensions to your organization. If you have a list, consider it a starting point. Actually, if surveys have been conducted in the past, there is an additional value in using the same areas. That allows you to compare results between surveys.

In the next chapter, you will be introduced to a number of techniques to use to identify the specific dimensions to survey, but for now, you need only provide a general description.

Return to the Employee Opinion Survey Planning Form (Figure 3-1). The last heading on the form is What to Survey. If you are planning a limited survey—a survey for just one or two areas of employment, write those titles beneath the heading What to Survey.

If you are going to survey a number of areas and know them, write their titles on the lines beneath the heading What to Survey.

If you want to survey most or all conditions of employment but have not specifically identified them, write something similar to:

> All conditions of employment

If you listed specific area titles, follow each with a one sentence definition. You may use the ones previously provided. If you are unsure as to a definition, procedures in the next chapter should obtain a definition for you.

At this point, you are not "locked in" to whatever you listed and defined, but you have a basic statement of what you will be surveying, and that will allow you to identify who to survey.

Who to Survey

To a large extent, who to survey is based on what you are surveying. The key consideration is to identify which employees have the needed information. Page 2 of the Employee Opinion Survey Planning Form is reproduced in Figure 4-1. It begins with the heading Who to Survey, and that is followed by two columns headed Grouping and Number.

Obviously, if you are surveying all conditions of employment and all employees, your determination of who to survey is complete. Under the heading, just write All Locations and All Employees. However, if you are not going to survey all employees, you need to identify which employees to include. You begin by considering location.

If your company has more than one location, to which locations do the areas to survey apply? If the areas to survey apply to more than one location, you generally want to include all those locations. Otherwise, locations omitted may question their omission, so if you are not including all relevant locations, have a reason and communicate that reason to the employees not included. You can be assured they will know the survey is being conducted at the other locations.

On separate sheets of paper, list the locations you have selected—one per sheet.

Next, identify the classifications of employees to survey. The classifications depend on what types of employees are in the workforce of your company. Typical classifications are:

Figure 4-1. Employee opinion survey planning form, page 2.

Who to Survey

Grouping   *Number*

When to Survey

Senior management or executive

Managers

Supervisors

Administrative and clerical

Professional

Sales

Hourly

Other possible groupings are full-time, part-time, permanent, and temporary.

If you are going to survey all employees at a location, write All Employees beneath that location. If you are not going to survey all classifications of employees at a location, write the classifications you are going to survey beneath that location.

The final step is to identify the number of employees in each group you have identified. Here, you want the total number of current employees. When you determine those numbers, write them opposite the appropriate classification. Be sure you have included all appropriate employees.

Now, transfer that information into the two columns on the form under the heading Who to Survey.

If you are surveying all employees at your company, and you have a total of 600 employees, that entry would appear as:

Who to Survey

Grouping	Number
All employees at all locations	600

If you have four locations and are surveying all employees at three of the locations, the entry might appear as:

Who to Survey

Grouping	Number
Location One—All Employees	200
Location Two—All Employees	150
Location Three—All Employees	250

If you are surveying all hourly and administrative and clerical employees at your company, that entry might appear as:

Who to Survey

Grouping	*Number*
All hourly employees at all locations	200
All administrative and clerical employees at all locations	100

If you are surveying all managers and supervisors at three of the locations, the entry might appear as:

Who to Survey

Grouping	*Number*
Location One	
All managers	30
All supervisors	60
Location Two	
All managers	25
All supervisors	55
Location Three	
All managers	35
All supervisors	65

At this point, you may decide that you cannot survey all the employees you have identified. Actually, you may not make such a final decision until you have developed the survey and know exactly how long it takes to complete. Even so, you should consider the possibility of using a sample of the total number of employees.

Sampling

To sample an employee population, you need to ensure that the sample reflects the entire population. This requires consideration of the size of the total population, unique characteristics of any portion of the total population, and the method used to select the sample.

Sample Size

The size of your sample will determine how confident you can be that the results represent the entire employee population from which the sample is drawn. For example, if you have an employee population of one hundred and use ninety in your sample, assuming they were selected to reflect the entire population, you can be fairly confident their responses reflect all employees. However, if you have one hundred employees and only sample two, chances are not too great that you have obtained responses that reflect the entire one hundred employees.

The factors to consider in order to determine the correct sample size are:

❑ *The Degree of Confidence.* This is a measure that refers to how confident you want to be that your results are not due to chance. The most used levels of confidence are .95 and .99. The higher the degree of confidence, the larger sample size is required. The degree of confidence selected will indicate the minimum sample size.

❑ *The Maximum Allowable Error.* This is the maximum error you will allow at the degree of confidence selected. Here, the less degree of error allowed, the larger the sample size required.

❑ *The Variations in the Employee Population.* The more homogeneous the employees are, the fewer employees are needed to be in the sample. You want to ensure your sample represents the full range of variations, or treat each significant variation as a separate group.

All of these are statistical considerations and their calculations are beyond the scope of this book. They represent the correct considerations in determining a sample size, but they require a professionally qualified person to perform the calculations. However, there are some general guidelines you can follow:

❑ *Identify the total group and any subgroups of employees to survey.* Here, in addition to the total employee population from whom you wish to obtain information, you should identify any subgroups that will tend to be similar and different from the entire employee population. For example, if a group of one hundred employees consists of sixty who speak English and forty who speak Spanish, you may want to classify them as two groups rather than one.

❏ *Determine the number needed from each group.* As a general guideline, you can use 5 percent of each group with a minimum of at least three employees. However, we have always preferred to use at least 10 percent and preferably 20 percent.

❏ *Select the number of employees required from each group.* In selecting employees for the sample, you want to ensure each employee in a group has an equal chance of being selected, so you will want to use some type of random selection technique.

Sampling Error

You may have noticed that published surveys often include a statement similar to:

Sampling error + − 3 or some other number. The sampling error indicates the deviation of results from the total population.

For example, assume you conducted an employee opinion survey with a group of 600 employees randomly selected from a population of 2,000 employees, and 60 percent of the employees surveyed indicated they were satisfied with the current benefit program. However, that 60 percent may not be exactly how all employees in the population might have responded. The sampling error calculation is a statistical calculation that estimates the deviation.

As with the earlier considerations of degree of confidence and maximum allowable error, the sampling is a calculation that should be made by someone with the proper training. The lower the sampling error, the more confidence one can have in the survey results.

Random Selection

One way to randomly select is to assign each employee in the population a number. Use consecutive numbers. Then use a published table of random numbers to select by number which employees should participate. (Random number tables are included in many statistics books.) Just be sure the table you use includes all the numbers you assigned.

Another method is to write each employee's name on a separate piece of paper, mix them, and then draw the number of names required. This approach can also be done with numbers rather than names.

A third method is to obtain a list of employees. Then select in a systematic fashion the number of names required. For example, assume you have one hundred employees and you want a sample of twenty. All you have to do is select every fifth name from the list.

The important point is to have a representative sample of the entire population and not to favor any one type of employee.

When to Survey

The last item on the planning form is When to Survey. In this initial planning, when refers to time of year—the date.

If surveys are conducted annually, you should stay with a date close to that of the previous survey unless there is a reason for a change. This assists in maintaining consistency and contributes to the ability to compare results between surveys.

If you are conducting a survey for the first time, give consideration to selecting a date that will lend itself to repeating in future years. Also, select a date when most employees are available. Consider employee vacations, busy times of the year, holidays, and any requirements unique to a location.

If you are conducting a limited survey or a survey prompted by a specific need, then determine a date that will provide the information when you need it, but again consider employee vacations, busy times of the year, and holidays.

If you will be surveying more than one location, it is generally best to survey them all at the same time. The greater the distance in time, the less confidence you can have in the consistency of results.

Enter the date by when you want the survey completed under the heading When to Survey. Later, you can calculate when the survey will have to be administered in order to be completed by that date.

Conclusion

You have now completed an initial plan for your survey. As you progress through this book, you will most probably revise it, but it is a starting point. In the next chapter, techniques will be introduced for determining exactly what conditions of employment areas to survey along with their subareas.

CHAPTER 5

SELECTING CONDITIONS OF EMPLOYMENT TO SURVEY

We live in a fantasy world, a world of illusion. The great task in life is to find reality.

IRIS MURDOCH,
The Times of London, April 15, 1983

In Chapter 4, an initial selection of areas to survey was completed as part of the planning process. This chapter describes techniques for identifying the conditions of employment applicable to your company. They then become the dimensions in which you will survey, but you also need to identify the subareas within each dimension.

At this point, you are ready to start gathering the information required for designing the survey, and that will require contact with employees. Before initiating such contact, the employees should be informed of the plan to design and conduct an employee opinion survey.

Initial Management Communication

The first communication should be to all management, so they are prepared to answer any employee questions. The media used should be the normal ones used for management communication. However, particularly with management, there is an advantage to communicating at a meeting, so answers to questions can be provided.

The points to cover are:

> The decision to have an employee opinion survey
>
> The objective of the survey
>
> When the survey will be conducted
>
> When results will be reported to all employees
>
> When individual members of management may be contacted for meetings or questionnaires to assist in identifying the conditions of employment to survey
>
> A statement that says: Employees will be told about the survey on _____
>
> Who to contact with questions

If an external consultant or consulting firm is being used, it should be mentioned that representatives from the firm will be gathering initial information for the survey design.

Initial Employee Communication

Shortly after communicating to management, a communication should be made to all employees. Again, use the normal media for communicating to them such as the employee newsletter, department meetings, e-mails, and memos. For example, a memo might say:

To all employees:

During October a survey of all employees will be conducted to obtain opinions of working conditions at our company. All of you will be asked to participate, and after tabulation, the results will be communicated throughout the company.

During the next month, information will be collected to identify the areas to survey. You may be asked to participate in a meeting or complete a questionnaire. If you are, your participation will assist in making the survey representative of our company.

If you have a question about the survey, you should contact your supervisor or the human resources department.

Once your employees know of the project, you are ready to begin, and having a starting point can be of considerable assistance.

A Starting Point

One approach is to develop a list of initial possible dimensions for the survey. Such a list can be obtained or developed from a number of sources:

Previous surveys

This book's list

Consultants or consulting firms

Published surveys

Employee handbooks

Company policies and procedures

A questionnaire

All of these can be used to create an initial list. They are discussed in detail below:

❑ *Previous Surveys.* For the reasons already mentioned, a consistency in employee opinion surveys is preferred, so if your company has conducted previous surveys, that should be your starting point. Identify the dimensions covered by the last survey. They may not be identified in the survey itself, but they should be described in the survey report. Make a list of these areas with their definitions if provided.

❑ *This Book's List.* Chapter 4 listed the conditions of employment we have been most often requested to survey, along with the definitions we normally use. You can use that list as a starting point.

☐ *Consultants or Consulting Firms*. Consultants and consulting firms who conduct employee opinion surveys can provide a list of the dimensions they most often survey. In some cases, they might have conducted an analysis at your company and can provide you with a list of areas from that project.

☐ *Published Surveys*. Employee opinion surveys for sale by publishers can be referenced for the areas they survey. Sometimes this information can also be obtained from marketing materials for the surveys. Published human resources textbooks may also include dimensions normally surveyed.

☐ *Employee Handbooks*. If your company publishes an employee handbook, it probably covers the conditions of employment at your company. A review of those chapter headings will provide an initial list.

☐ *Company Policies and Procedures*. The company's human resources policies and procedures are another source. There is generally a policy and procedure for each condition of employment.

☐ *A Questionnaire*. Another approach is to use a questionnaire to obtain input for an initial list of conditions of employment. It can be sent to a sample of senior managers, managers, supervisors, and nonmanagement employees. Since you are only seeking a starting point, it is not necessary to question a large sample. You can consider as few as two to four from each group. Just be sure you have all locations represented.

A sample questionnaire is illustrated in Figure 5-1. It also appears on the accompanying disk.

When you receive all the questionnaires, use up to the twenty most frequently mentioned conditions of employment as your starting list.

A Word of Caution

A study was conducted by a Michigan university to determine what areas should be included in a standard employee opinion survey it was planning to publish. Questionnaires were sent to 100 executives. Seventy-four were returned. In total, there were 322 different areas described, but there were only 7 that could be said to have any consistently significant rating.

Figure 5-1. Employee opinion survey questionnaire.

To: _____

We are currently in the process of developing an employee opinion survey. Its purpose will be to identify employee perceptions regarding conditions of employment at our company.

To assist in this effort, we are sending a questionnaire to a number of employees. Please take a few moments and answer the following questions. Then return the completed questionnaire to _____.
We need to receive all completed questionnaires by _____.

What areas and conditions of employment do you feel should be surveyed to determine how employees perceive working at our company? Please list the areas on the lines below.

Number   Area

(continues)

Figure 5-1 *(continued)*

Once you have listed all the areas you feel should be surveyed, enter a number on the short line in front of each area you identified. The number should indicate how important you feel each area is to an overall evaluation of our company. Use a 3 to indicate the area is very important to an evaluation of our company's conditions of employment, a 2 to indicate the area is important to an evaluation of our company's conditions of employment, and a 1 to indicate the area is not too important to an evaluation of our company's conditions of employment.

Now, write one of the three numbers on the short line in front of each area.

With that accomplished, you have completed the questionnaire. Your responses will be combined with those from other employees, and a final list developed for our employee opinion survey.

The university decided to follow up with telephone interviews. What they discovered was that most participants had very strong views of what areas in a company environment were important, but few could provide any basis for their perceptions.

Some obtained their lists from textbooks; some from consultants; some from professional associations. The university finally created a list and sent it to the participants for approval. That approach, similar to the one we are suggesting, worked, and a final list of 24 areas was developed.

The point of this story is to be aware that many people have a list of areas to which they may ascribe, but these are areas that were not determined though any type of empirical information collected within the company.

Starting List

Once you have a starting list, you may want to make some adjustments. Review the list, and if it seems complete, you are ready for the next step, but if it seems to have omitted an important area, add it. Also, if you feel one of the areas is no longer applicable to your company, remove it.

An example of a conditions of employment form is shown in Figure 5-2. There are three columns headed: Ranking, Dimension, and Definition. Completing one of these forms gives you an initial document to use in finalizing the areas to survey.

Review the areas you have initially identified. You are going to write them on the lines in the Dimension column and follow each with its definition. However, you do not want to list them in any order that implies sequence of application or value—importance—so using your own judgment, mix the order of the items before listing. Then list them on the form along with their definitions. Leave the ranking lines blank.

Each item should appear similar to:

Conditions of Employment

Ranking	Dimension	Definition
_____	Compensation	The cash rewards an employee receives for performing her job.

With this form completed, you have a starting point. However, if you are unable to develop an initial list, you need to conduct an analysis within your company. We review how to do that later in this chapter. At this point, assume you have a list and are ready to have the appropriate employees within your company participate in arriving at a final identification of areas to survey.

Figure 5-2. Conditions of employment.

Ranking	Dimension	Definition

Figure 5-3 *(continued)*

When you are satisfied that all conditions have been identified, indicate how important you feel each one is to be part of the survey. You can indicate that by writing a number on the short line in front of each bold area. Use the following numbers:

3 Very important

2 Important

1 Not too important

When you have completed this survey, please return it to _____. We need to have all returned no later than _____.

___ **Immediate Supervision**—the direction, planning, and control exercised by the individual to whom you report

___ **Job Assignment**—the responsibilities and authorities of the job you are asked to perform

___ **Communication**—the communication you receive and provide

___ **Performance Measurement**—the evaluation of your individual job performance

___ **Compensation**—the cash rewards you receive for your work

___ **Benefits**—the noncash rewards you receive for your work

___ **Job Security**—the confidence you have in your safety and continuation of employment

___ **Executive Management**—the leadership, planning, and control exercised by the senior executives of the company

___ **Equal Treatment**—the fair and nondiscriminatory treatment you and other employees receive

___ **Training**—the training provided for your current job, changes to your job, and future jobs

___ **Career Opportunities**—the opportunities to increase your responsibilities and grow within the company

___ **Facilities**—the environment in which you work and the availability of necessary equipment and supplies

___ **Overall Company**—all the things that contribute to the company and its operations

(continues)

From Whom to Seek Information

If there is a specific request from someone or some group to con
survey, that individual or group is the one to contact. If the sur
be a general one, you need to contact a wider variety of people.

Generally, representatives of senior management, middle
ment, supervisors, human resources, and nonmanagement emplo
contacted for information. Then, sampling techniques are emp
determine the number of each to contact using the following
tion-gathering methods: questionnaires, interviews, meetings, o
bination of one or more.

Questionnaires

A questionnaire is the most efficient method to finalize your li
cially if you have a large population or a number of geographic l
Questionnaires allow many people to participate and are inexp
create, administer, and tabulate.

If you used a questionnaire to develop your initial list, you
do not want to send a second questionnaire to the same people.
allow you to involve more employees in the development proc

An example of a typical survey questionnaire is shown in F
It uses the areas and definitions introduced in the previous cha
also available on the accompanying disk.

Figure 5-3. Employee opinion dimension identification survey.

To: _____

Our company is in the process of creating an employee opini
Its purpose will be to discover the perceptions of our employe
ing the conditions of employment at our company. Your as
requested to assist in identifying the conditions to survey.

A number of possible employment conditions have been ide
defined. They appear below in bold letters. Read them and tl
tions. If you feel any should not be included as the basis for
cross them off. If you feel some should be added, write their
the lines at the end of the list along with a short definition.

Figure 5-3 *(continued)*

Interviews

An interview generally requires between thirty minutes and an hour. It often is identical to the questionnaire, only the instructions are provided by the interviewer. A list of conditions of employment similar to that portion of the questionnaire should be completed in advance for use at the interview.

Since the interviewer can only handle one person at a time, the interview is a more time-consuming approach. Frequently, it is limited to representatives of senior management.

The outcome of the interview should be the same as that of the questionnaire.

Meetings

When you have a number of people from whom to obtain information on the same subject, a meeting is often the most efficient method. Just be sure the participants are at the same level within the organization and have the same degree of knowledge.

Meeting Format and Results

The following is a guide that can be used to lead such a meeting. The guide consists of two different styles of printing. The italicized text is a suggested script for the leader. The traditional text represents directions.

Meeting Guide

The meeting is meant to be conducted in a conference setting. Two chart pads with markers are required. Also required is the list of conditions of employment and their definitions for each participant along with note-taking pads and pencils.

We are here today to determine the areas that will serve as a basis for our company's employee opinion survey. The survey will be conducted to discover the opinions of our employees regarding conditions of employment.

A number of areas have been suggested. Our task is to review those areas and make any change we feel is required.

Let's begin by each of you reviewing the conditions of employment that have already been suggested.

Distribute a list of those areas to each participant. Then read the titles and their definitions.

If you feel any should not be included as the basis for our survey, cross them off.

Give them a moment to do this.

Now, if you feel some should be added, write their names on the lines at the end of the list along with a short definition.

Give them a moment to do this.

Now, indicate how important you feel each one is to be part of the survey. You can indicate that by writing a number on the short line in front of each bold area. Use a 3 for the areas you feel are very important; a 2 for the areas you feel are important; and a 1 for areas you feel are not too important.

Give them time to do this. It may require five to ten minutes.

When they have completed this, say:

You have just rated possible areas to use as a basis for our employee opinion survey. Now you are going to meet in small groups and as groups, arrive at ratings for these conditions of employment.

You are to place the conditions of employment into groups that represent the three ratings.

It is important in your group work to express your feelings and discuss any differences, so do not make it a mathematical activity. Do not add your ratings and divide by the number in your group. That is not what the exercise is about.

Divide them into groups and start the process. Circulate among the groups as they work.

There is no specific time limit for this assignment, but it usually requires between ten and fifteen minutes.

When the groups have completed the assignment, reconvene the entire group.

Have each group read its decisions for the first category (Very Important). As they do, write these on a chart pad or board. Repeat the procedure for the other two categories, each on a separate sheet of chart paper for each group. Post the charts so all three can be seen at one time.

So, what you have done is first individually rate the conditions of employment as to their importance for an employee opinion survey.

Then, in small groups, you discussed and arrived at group decisions regarding their importance.

If the categories are the same, you can move on to the conclusion of the session. If there are differences, you need to resolve them by discussion.

Accomplish that through the use of overhead questions (questions asked of the entire group rather than individuals). However, it may take a minute or two before you receive a response. Ask for the basis for conflicting ratings of the same conditions of employment. If the group does not decide through discussion, have them vote.

Continue with this process (without a break) until all are in agreement as to the categories.

You have now categorized the conditions of employment for the employee opinion survey. The questions on the survey will be based on these categories and degrees of importance.

If you have time, you can have the group identify the three most significant subareas of each condition of employment. For example, Compensation might include annual reviews, job evaluations, and methods of pay. You can have the participants indicate the importance of each of these subareas using the following three categories:

1. Very Important

2. Important

3. Not Too Important

If you have limited time, identify the subareas for just the Very Important category items. Check for questions.

Other Approaches

Sometimes, more than one approach is used. For example, interviews may be held to develop an initial list. Then a meeting may be held to finalize the list and final questionnaires sent to involve all.

There are also numerous other techniques and devices that can be used to identify areas to survey. Some of these may be internally developed; some used by external firms and consultants; some available as published devices. Any are acceptable as long as they produce the information required and do so in a valid and reliable approach.

Combining Results

Once you have collected all of the inputs regarding areas to survey and their relative value, they need to be combined to determine a final list. This is relatively simple if you feel all sources provided the same value of information. Here, you only need to identify frequencies of responses and the numerical value for each.

A form for combining responses is shown in Figure 5-4. The procedure is to begin with the responses from one person or group. List those responses in the first column of the form. List those with a 3 rating first. Then list the 2's, and finally the 1's. Write the appropriate evaluation numbers after each area in the second column.

Figure 5-4. Area results combining form.

Area	1	2	3	Average

Next, take the second person or group's responses. Where there are similar responses, write the appropriate importance number after the area in the third column. If the second set identified areas the first one did not, add those areas in the first column after the first set of responses and write the importance numbers in the third column. However, leave the importance number lines in the second column blank. If the second set of responses did not have all the areas the first one did, leave the importance number lines following those areas blank in the third column.

Continue in this manner until you have entered all sets of responses. Our sample form only has columns for three sets of responses, so you may have to use more than one form or revise the one provided.

When you have all responses entered, total and divide by the number of responses for each specific area. That is the average and it is entered in the Average column on the form. Not all areas may have responses from all people so be sure to only divide by the number of responses you have for each condition of employment. Figure 5-5 shows a completed sample form.

If you are dealing with separate locations, you should complete one of these forms for each location. That will allow you to identify any conditions of employment that may only be applicable to some locations. That could require you to have separate versions of the survey.

Generally, you will be combining inputs from all employees regardless of classifications. However, in some instances you may feel that inputs have different weights due to their knowledge of conditions of employees' employment. In those situations, you may want to weight each group's input.

For example, if one group has more information and involvement with conditions of employment such as human resources, you might use their numbers as given, but for a group with less knowledge, you might reduce their input.

One company used the following adjustments:

Human resources	100%
Senior managers	80%
Managers	75%
Supervisors	90%
Nonmanagement employees	60%

These numbers reflect that company's evaluation of the degrees of

Figure 5-5. Sample area results combining form.

Area	1	2	3	Average
Compensation	3	3	3	3
Benefits	3	3	3	3
Job Security	3	2	3	2.7
Job Satisfaction	3	3	3	3
Supervision	3	3	3	3
Equal Treatment	3	2	2	2.3
Career Opportunities	2		3	2.5
Training	2	2	2	2
Company Image	2	1		1.5
Executive Management	2			2
Environment		1	1	1
Safety		3		3
Quality		2	3	2.5

conditions of employment knowledge each classification had. If you feel you need some type of adjustment percentage, you will have to determine what is appropriate at your company. Figure 5-6 shows an information combination form. It can be used to combine responses when adjustment percents are used. The form also appears on the accompanying disk.

The form allows you to enter the numbers from two sources along with the values you have assigned each. For example, the same form appears in Figure 5-7 with areas and values added for two groups: human resources and managers.

In the example, the average for each group is shown in the Number column opposite the Item (in this case, a condition of employment). The Value column has the value assigned to the group's average response. The value for the human resources was 100 percent (or 1 as shown on the form). The value for the managers was 70 percent (or 0.7 as shown on the form).

The next step is to multiply the numbers for each group by its assigned value and enter the result in the Result column for each group. That has been accomplished on the form that appears in Figure 5-8.

The final step is to calculate the average of the two groups' Results, so you add the two Result figures for each competency and divide by two since there are two groups. That has been done on the example shown in Figure 5-9.

Whether you averaged inputs or adjusted them before averaging, you have a list of conditions of employment with a rating number. The next step is to list the conditions of employment in a descending order based on their final average numbers. List the highest numbers first.

With the list completed, review it to determine if there are any conditions of employment that should be added. Sometimes, there is a specific issue to survey. Other times, one may be missed. Then have the final list reviewed and approved by whoever requested the survey. This will be the basis for the survey. Its results will be in these areas, so ensure this will meet the requested needs of the company.

Conclusion

Once the list is approved, you are ready to develop the survey questions and approach. That begins with the next chapter in which the subareas for each condition of employment will be identified.

Figure 5-6. Information combination form.

Group: _____   **Group:** _____

Item	Number	Value	Result	Number	Value	Result	Total

Figure 5-7. Information combination form (areas and values added).

Group: Human Resources _____   **Group: Managers** _____

Item	Number	Value	Result	Number	Value	Result	Total
Leadership	15	1		17	0.7		
Oral Communication	12	1		10	0.7		
Planning	10	1		15	0.7		
Decision Making	9	1		11	0.7		

Figure 5-8. Information combination form (results).

Group: Human Resources _____ **Group: Managers** _____

Item	Number	Value	Result	Number	Value	Result	Total
Leadership	15	1	15	17	0.7	11.9	
Oral Communication	12	1	12	10	0.7	7.0	
Planning	10	1	10	15	0.7	10.6	
Decision Making	9	1	9	11	0.7	7.7	

Figure 5-9. Information combination form (average results).

Group: Human Resources _____   **Group: Managers** _____

Item	Number	Value	Result	Number	Value	Result	Total
Leadership	15	1		17	0.7	11.9	13.5
Oral Communication	12	1		10	0.7	7.0	9.6
Planning	10	1		15	0.7	10.6	10.2
Decision Making	9	1		11	0.7	7.7	8.3

CHAPTER 6

DEVELOPING EMPLOYEE SURVEY DEMOGRAPHICS

I guess there are two schools of thought about this—yours and mine.

ERNEST GALLO,
The New York Times, May 2, 1988

There are times when all that is required from an employee opinion survey is a single collective response from all employees, but those times tend to be few and far between. More often, information is needed from different groups of employees in order to fully understand their opinions.

A North Carolina manufacturing plant surveyed all 400 of its employees. One of the dimensions on the survey was performance reviews. Over 70 percent of all employees reported being satisfied with the company's performance review system, but when responses were reported by department, positive satisfaction with the performance review system ranged from 20 percent to 90 percent.

If the company in the example had not reported by department, it could have been under a false assumption that everything was fine. That could have resulted in a major surprise in the future.

The following is another example of the types of variations that can be attributed to employee groupings. These are responses to a survey inquiry regarding job assignment. They are reported for total employees and ten groupings. Each group is reported as a percent of that group providing both positive and negative responses. The table presents results from a small engine manufacturing firm's survey.

Question: How fairly are job assignments handled in your work area?

Employee Group	Number of Employees	Positive Responses	Negative Responses
All Employees	1,000	70%	30%
Males	600	92%	8%
Females	400	38%	62%
African-American	200	50%	50%
Native American	100	75%	25%
Hispanic	200	50%	50%
Caucasian	100	75%	25%
Asian	400	88%	12%
Main office	200	75%	25%
Plant 1	300	33%	67%
Plant 2	500	90%	10%

Here again, the overall report statistic was misleading, and the demographic reports identified groups of employees who differed significantly from the overall average in their satisfaction with job assignments.

Being able to report by various employee groupings usually provides valuable insights, so you want to be able to identify those groups. However, you should not attempt to identify specific survey responses with individual employees.

Individual Identification

Most written and computer employee opinion surveys do not request individual identification, although they often include an optional opportunity for any employee who wishes to be identified. The theory is that you will receive more open and truthful responses if the participants can remain anonymous.

A Rhode Island–based company conducted a survey to identify supervisory problems. It felt the information would only be useful if it could be identified with specific supervisors, but it also felt the information would be best if offered without identification.

The survey it distributed had no identifying questions, and the introduction stated it was to be completed without individual identification. However, the company had coded the surveys with a bar code placed as inconspicuously as possible within the survey document.

The company was correct. The responses were very revealing and identified specific problem supervisors. A number of employees completing the survey recognized the bar codes for what they were, and soon everyone at the company knew the surveys had been coded.

The company defended its actions but was never again able to conduct a meaningful survey. In fact, from that point, it experienced continual problems getting employees to believe any of its communications.

You do not want to do anything like this or use hidden identification such as pinpricking a code into each questionnaire. If it is really important to identify individual employees with their responses, either say so and leave the name optional, or say so and request the name.

An Illinois company included an essay question at the conclusion of its survey. The question asked for recommendations to improve efficiency. The survey did not ask for identifying information, but it requested each employee to write a word or number on their survey, so each recommendation had an identifier.

After reviewing the survey, the company selected what it thought was a good number of recommendations, but in most cases, it needed additional information. The code words and numbers from those surveys were published, and the employees were asked to identify themselves. Seventy-eight percent of the employees did.

Employee Groupings

Being able to report the survey results by employee groupings is important, but to do so, you need to identify the groupings required in advance. Then appropriate questions can be included in the survey, but there are two cautions:

> Don't require such detailed demographics that employees will feel they can be individually identified.

> Don't request demographic information unless you are going to use it.

Don't Require Such Detailed Demographics That Employees Feel They Can Be Individually Identified

Assume you want to be able to provide reports by length of service, gender, race, and educational level—all legitimate employee groupings—so you request that information. If you request that information and also department identification and your departments consist of only a few people, it may appear that you are attempting to identify specific employees or, if not attempting to do so, at least are capable of it.

Don't Request Demographic Information Unless You Are Going to Use It

Although demographic information is usually of assistance in interpreting survey results, if you are not going to use it, don't request it. It will eventually become apparent that you do not use the information, and it then raises a question as to why you want it.

Typical Demographic Groupings

The most typical demographic groupings used are:

> Employee classification
>
> Department
>
> Length of service
>
> Race
>
> Gender
>
> Age
>
> Location—if employees are from more than one location

Less frequently requested are:

> Education
>
> Marital status
>
> Length of department service
>
> Length of service in current position

Past Survey Demographics

If your company has previously conducted employee opinion surveys, be sure to review the demographics the past surveys requested and reported. These two are not always the same. Sometimes demographic information is requested but not used to report results. If that has occurred, question why, but give consideration to using at least the same demographics as past surveys. As with all survey results, it provides a basis for comparisons.

Considerations

There are several considerations to keep in mind as you identify the demographic groups. Already mentioned was to avoid any groupings that appear to be ways to identify individuals; only ask for areas you will use, and only ask for areas applicable to your company.

Another consideration concerns equal treatment of employees. It is generally illegal to make employment decisions based on nonjob-required information such as race, sex, marital status, or military service. So if you identify any of these characteristics, use them solely to interpret survey results. Do not use any of this information to make employment decisions regarding an individual employee. However, this may be an area you should review with your employment attorney.

Another area you may wish to review with your attorney is the surveying of employees covered by a collective bargaining agreement. Be sure you have the right to conduct the survey; that is, if you have to obtain the union's agreement or review the survey with the union.

Even more crucial is checking with an employment attorney about conducting a survey of employees who are subjects of a union-organizing campaign or election. Doing so in such a situation may very possibly be interpreted as an unfair labor practice.

Identifying Your Employee Demographics

Figure 6-1 shows an employee demographic identification form. It has two columns: Demographic and Identification. In the Demographic column, list the demographic areas for which you wish to receive survey reports. List only those that you feel can make a contribution to your overall survey objective.

Then review the following information for the demographics you selected, and determine which type of identification will best fit your company. Enter that identifying information in the Identification column beside each demographic.

Figure 6-1. Demographic identification form.

Demographic   Identification

Employee Classification

Different classifications of employees are used at different companies. You want to select the ones applicable to your company, and you want to select groupings for which there are different conditions of employment such as pay practices, overtime, work schedules, and benefits.

Typical classifications are:

> Executive
>
> Management
>
> Supervisory
>
> Administrative and Clerical
>
> Sales
>
> Professional
>
> Hourly
>
> Temporary
>
> Permanent
>
> Full-Time
>
> Part-Time

Not all of the above classifications are used for any one company. Sometimes only exempt and nonexempt classifications are used. Also, if any of your employees are covered by a labor contract, they should be considered as a separate group.

Keep in mind, you are going to be asking for this information on the survey, so you want to use classifications the employees understand.

A company in Arkansas decided the ability to receive survey reports by exempt and nonexempt employee groupings would be helpful, so they asked for that type of identification on the survey. Unfortunately, the employees had no idea what those terms meant. Most of them left the question unanswered.

Department

Department identification can provide excellent information and is important when communicating survey results through individual supervisors. Specific assignments and supervisors often make a significant difference in perceptions. As a guideline, do not request this identification for departments of fewer than ten people. If you do and also request other information, it may appear you are attempting to identify individual employees.

If you have department numbers, you can use them. However, in many situations employees do not know their department numbers or the correct names of their departments. Whatever you decide as an identifier requires the employee to be able to respond.

A Kansas financial services company gave each employee a card as they arrived to participate in its group-administered written survey. The card had the employee's name, classification, and department number on it, so the employee was able to refer to it when completing the survey.

Length of Service

Some companies refer to this as seniority, and other companies use various lengths of service for different purposes. This is often one of the most useful groupings for reports, but again you want to be confident your employees will be able to correctly respond. In determining how to measure length of service, it is generally easier to supply ranges rather than request specific numbers of years. That can simplify tabulation and appears to be less usable for individual identification.

If you use ranges, select ones that are meaningful to your company. For example, if you are only interested in employees with lengths of service greater or less than fifteen years, you could only offer two ranges:

Less than fifteen years

Fifteen years and over

However, if you want to know the exact number of years for each employee, you could ask something similar to:

How many years of service do you have with our company?

In what year were you born?

If there are significant changes in working conditions at certain lengths of service, use those points. For example, if there is vesting or an increase in compensation at a certain length of service, you may want to use that as a break point. Also, if your company has only been in existence ten years, having ranges in excess of ten years is unnecessary.

Whatever you decide to ask, be sure it can be tabulated. That is something which is discussed in greater detail in a later chapter.

Race and Gender

Using these two groupings sometimes seems to bother employees, so if they are used, be sure to explain why. Both can provide valuable information regarding different perceptions in such areas as equal treatment and job assignments.

Age

Like length of service, age is best requested in ranges. Also, it should reflect your company, so only use ranges that are applicable.

Location

If you are using departments for identification, that may automatically allow you to identify groups by geographic location. If it doesn't or if you are not using departments, you should identify by location if there is more than one. This again is a grouping that can often provide significant information regarding differences in employee satisfaction.

Other Possible Groupings

Other demographics should be used only when there is a specific reason to report in such a manner. If there is a reason to assume a significant difference in employee perceptions, such as an apparent problem between supervisors and newly hired college graduates, you may want to report by educational level.

In some companies, "length of department service" and "length of service in current position" may relate to specific working conditions such as job assignment, overtime, and vacation date selection. These are conditions that may impact satisfaction, so in such instances, they might be included as appropriate demographic groupings.

There also may be other categories unique to your company. We have conducted surveys with such categories as:

> Driver's license
>
> Language ability
>
> Assigned shift
>
> Veteran status

But in each instance, there was a specific reason for including the category, and each category had a significant enough population to make a group.

Typical Questions

Once you have identified the demographic groupings and the specifics of each, you can then develop the demographic identification questions to include in the survey. The following questions are typical:

> Of which employee group are you?
>
> ❏ Executive
> ❏ Management
> ❏ Supervisor
> ❏ Professional
> ❏ Administrative and Clerical
> ❏ Production

Are you:

- ❏ A full-time employee?
- ❏ A part-time employee?

What is the three-digit code for your department?

_____

What is your gender?

- ❏ Male
- ❏ Female

What is your race?

- ❏ African-American
- ❏ Asian
- ❏ Hispanic
- ❏ Native American
- ❏ Middle Eastern
- ❏ Caucasian

What is your length of service?

- ❏ Under six months
- ❏ Over six months, but less than one year
- ❏ Over one year, but less than three years
- ❏ Over three years, but less than ten years
- ❏ Over ten years, but less than fifteen years
- ❏ Over fifteen years, but less than twenty-five years
- ❏ Over twenty-five years

What is your age group?

- ❏ 16 to 20
- ❏ 21 to 25
- ❏ 26 to 35

❏ 36 to 45

❏ 46 to 55

❏ 56 to 65

❏ Over 65

Location in the Survey

So where should such questions be located in the survey? Generally, they are positioned as the first items, but, on occasion, they are positioned as the last item. By placing them first, it immediately communicates to the participants what identifying information is required. If they are the final items, the instructions should mention that such information will be requested at the conclusion of the survey but that it will be used only for reporting by employee groups.

Participation Control

Although you generally do not want to identify surveys by individual, you do need some type of control to ensure each employee has an opportunity to complete a survey (and only one survey). That means some type of record is required. How to maintain that control varies by type of survey format.

Group- and Individually Administered Written Surveys

Group-administered surveys can be controlled by ensuring who attends each group session. You can require some identification (personal recognition in a small organization or identification badges in a large one). As someone participates, her name is either recorded or crossed off a list of employees eligible to participate in the survey. No surveys are allowed to be removed from the room. If someone must leave for some reason, he cannot take his survey with him.

In an earlier example, the distribution of cards to employees with specific information such as department number and job classification was mentioned. This can also be used as a control device.

In that procedure, a card is produced for each employee with that employee's information on it. When the employee arrives at the location, the card is given to him. The employee refers to it in answering the demographic questions, and a separate basket is located for the employee to discard the card after use. This ensures that each employee only completes one survey, and it records who did and did not participate.

This same approach can be used with individual written surveys.

Written Mailed Surveys

These are easier to control as far as distribution. One survey is mailed to each employee. However, there is an element of the process that is more difficult to control: reproduction of the survey. Some organizations use a form that is nonreproducible, but with improved copying techniques that is becoming more difficult. Some imprint the survey form with a seal or hologram that is difficult to copy. Others allow a very short time for completion and return. Some companies use a numbered envelope, but this does have the disadvantage of implying the ability to determine exactly from whom a completed survey is received.

These are some of the reasons we prefer to administer a written survey to groups or individuals at a company location rather than mail it.

Online Surveys

In programming a survey for online use, a control methodology can be incorporated. For example, an employee can be required to enter a password or control number to complete a survey. This is similar to having to enter a password for e-mail. However, if the number used is an existing one assigned to the employee, it may be perceived as attempting to identify the employee with her responses.

This can be avoided by using some type of randomly supplied numbers. For example, a company could prepare numbered cards. Each card would be prepared with a different number, and the total number of cards would equal the total number of employees. The numbers used do not have to be in consecutive order, or you can use alphanumeric codes.

The cards are distributed in some random manner. Sometimes, employees draw from a group of cards. Other times, groups of cards are sent to a department in sealed envelopes and randomly distributed.

The online survey is programmed for allowing each of the numbers to participate in the survey but only one time. Such an approach controls the online survey participation even if the survey is available on a personal computer at a nonwork location.

Interviews and Focus Meetings

These formats by their very nature identify the participants. Participants are selected and scheduled. Sometimes, as with group completion of a written survey, a record is made of those attending a focus group, but the person conducting the group does not know or ask for participant names.

Conclusion

With the demographic groupings identified and their identifying questions prepared, you are ready to develop the survey questions. That is the subject of the next chapter.

PART TWO

DEVELOPING YOUR EMPLOYEE OPINION SURVEY

7

DESIGNING SURVEY QUESTIONS

Get to know what you don't know as fast as you can.

ROBERT HELLER,
The Super Manager

With your survey dimensions and employee reporting demographics determined, you are now ready to develop your actual survey questions. A key guideline for the questions is a determination of how many to include.

Number of Survey Questions

If you are conducting a survey in only one dimension, there may be only a few questions, but for a survey dealing with eight or more dimensions, the number of questions becomes a time consideration.

For example, assume you have identified ten dimensions you want to survey. You also have six questions of employee demographic information and a concluding essay question. You want the average employee to complete the survey in fifty minutes, so you can schedule sixty minutes for the survey with ten minutes for those who may require additional time.

The only method for knowing exactly how long it will take a typical employee to answer your questions is to have the questions answered by a group of employees and then calculate their average time. However, there also are some general guidelines you can use.

Assuming you are using objective or multiple-choice response questions, and you have identified six demographic areas, the introduction and instructions will probably require five minutes, the six demographic questions will require two minutes, and the final essay question will probably take two minutes.

Once again, use the following suggested times:

Introduction and instructions	five minutes
Six demographic questions	two minutes
Final essay question	two minutes
Total	**nine minutes**

When you subtract these nine minutes from the desired fifty minutes to complete the entire survey, you are left with forty-one minutes for the survey questions in the ten dimensions you identified. That is 4.1 minutes or 246 seconds per dimension. A typical multiple-choice or objective question generally requires ten seconds to answer, so that means you have time for 24.6 questions per dimension (246 divided by ten) and 246 total questions (24.6 times ten). These two numbers now become guidelines for developing your questions.

If you are surveying overall satisfaction and importance for each dimension, two questions per dimension will be required, leaving 22.6 questions for each dimension.

If you elect to use a different time objective, more or fewer dimensions, or more or fewer essay questions, it will change the number of question guidelines. Later in this chapter, a form and instructions will lead you through calculations for your survey. First, you need to decide the type of questions to use, and to a large extent that depends on the type of responses you request. For that decision, you have to consider:

Survey format

Tabulation method

Survey Format

The various formats described will determine the responses you can offer, but our recommendation is to use, as a base survey, either a written or an online format. To a large extent, both of these formats use similar questions. You can use any of the question types described. Interviews and focus groups are able to use just about any type of response. Interviews often use the same questions as written and online surveys, but interviews provide an opportunity to probe for additional information. Those probing questions usually have to be created during the interview and require a skilled interviewer.

Focus group questions are answered through group discussion. This limits the number that can be asked and the format they take. As with interviews, focus groups should be conducted by someone skilled in their operation.

Tabulation Method

Tabulation method also relates to the compiling and reporting of survey results. If multiple-choice, objective, and any other types of questions requesting numerical answers are used, they can be readily tabulated and reported. For example, if eighty participants out of one hundred total participants answer yes to a question and twenty answer no, it is easy to tabulate and report that 80 percent answered yes and 20 percent answered no.

Fill-in and essay questions are more difficult and time-consuming to tabulate. They have to be read and interpreted. This also brings into the mix the "tabulator's" perceptions.

Depending on their design, interview and focus group responses are usually summarized and reported by the person conducting them. However, like fill-in and essay questions, they often require some degree of interpretation by the interviewer and leader.

The recommendation of this book is to use written and online surveys. Online surveys can be programmed to offer and tabulate a wide variety of responses for each question. For example, there can be a different number of alternatives or a different scale for each multiple-choice question. Online surveys have few limitations imposed by the method; even so we recommend multiple-choice questions.

Multiple-choice questions are also the recommendation for written surveys. They are relatively easy for participants to answer and easy to tabulate and report. However, they can pose some limitations on responses.

If the survey responses are hand-tabulated, the response formats can vary. If the responses are computer-scanned and -tabulated, they can also vary, provided the tabulation program is written specifically for the survey. However, in many cases a standard program or an external service is used for the tabulation. In those instances, the responses must fit the pre-programmed format.

For example, a typical tabulation program is based on a certain number of alternatives for each question (three, four, and five are quite common). Assume you are using a five-response program. That means you can use a standard answer sheet that offers five possible responses to each question, but that also means you cannot use questions that require more than five responses.

Now, let's examine the questions to use and their response alternatives.

Response Alternatives

Earlier in this book several basic question types were described: objective, multiple choice, ranking, essay, and fill-in. Responses to the first three types can be recorded in a similar fashion. The alternative answers for each question can be provided, and the participant just needs to indicate the one selected. Essay and fill-in questions are a different matter and will be dealt with later.

Objective questions generally require two possible responses: yes and no. However, don't know or not applicable is sometimes provided as a third possible response.

Multiple-choice questions offer several possible responses, but how many? With an online survey, it can be as many as can be displayed on the screen and programmed. With a written survey that is computer-scanned and -tabulated, there may be a limitation. However, in most cases five alternative responses can be used.

Response Scales

A convenient method for recording employee opinion survey responses is to use a multiple-choice scale. Typically, it is a scale of four or five points. However, there are scales with as few as three points and some with as many as nine or ten points. For example, the following is a typical employee opinion survey question followed by a five-point scale for response:

> How satisfied are you with the training you received for your current job?

Below is a five-point scale that can be used for answering such a question:

Very Satisfied	Somewhat Satisfied	Neither Satisfied nor Dissatisfied	Somewhat Dissatisfied	Very Dissatisfied
5	4	3	2	1

If responses are being marked in the survey, the appropriate number can be circled on the printed scale. If answered on a separate answer sheet, an identified space can be marked. Some answer sheets use letters for responses. If that is your situation, the scale is furnished with letters as here:

Very Satisfied	Somewhat Satisfied	Neither Satisfied nor Dissatisfied	Somewhat Dissatisfied	Very Dissatisfied
A	B	C	D	E

If you use a numerical scale for responses, we have found it to be most effective when it consists of at least three possible responses: high, middle, and low. However, a scale offering five alternative points seems to work best. Employees seem more comfortable with it. They do not have to use the end points, so they usually ignore them and answer most questions with the middle three numbers.

Some survey designers prefer a seven- or nine-point scale, and others prefer to allow decimals or fractions.

A five-point scale is basically still a three-point scale. There are three positions: the mid- or neutral point (3), above the midpoint (4 and 5), and below the midpoint (1 and 2). Adding numbers merely allows for a degree of above or below the midpoint.

For example, using the above five-point scale, 1 and 2 are both dissatisfied responses. 1 is just more dissatisfied than 2, and 4 and 5 are both more than satisfied responses.

Some survey designers prefer an even-numbered scale—a scale with no neutral midpoint. The reasoning often stated is that an even-numbered scale forces the participant to make a positive or negative decision since there is no neutral position. Our experience with even-numbered scales is that they tend to skew responses to the positive side, so we prefer an odd-numbered scale.

There are five basic scales that we use in employee opinion surveys: satisfaction, importance, rating, amount, and agreement. The satisfaction scale was introduced above. It is for responses to questions that begin with:

How satisfied are you with . . .

The importance scale is similar:

Very Important	Somewhat Important	Neither Important nor Unimportant	Somewhat Unimportant	Very Unimportant
5	4	3	2	1

The importance scale is for responses to questions that begin with:

How important to you is . . .

The rating scale is:

Excellent	Very Good	Typical	Fair	Poor
A	B	C	D	E

The rating scale is for responses to questions that begin with:

How do you rate . . .

The amount scale is for responses to statements such as:

The amount of work I am requested to do is . . .

Much Too Much	Too Much	Just Right	Too Little	Much Too Little
A	B	C	D	E

The amount scale is for indicating the degree of agreement with statements such as:

The amount of work I am requested to do is . . .

The agreement scale is used to respond to statements rather than questions. It is:

Strongly Agree	Agree	Neither Agree nor Disagree	Disagree	Strongly Disagree
5	4	3	2	1

Instructions for its use are:

> Read the following statement and then indicate how well you agree or disagree with it.

Using one of these scales allows you to group similar questions. For example, you can group together all the questions asking about satisfaction, all the questions asking about importance, all the questions asking for a rating, and all the statements to agree or disagree with. For example:

> Using the provided scale, indicate your agreement to the following questions:
>
> I feel my company has an excellent reputation in the community.
>
> My supervisor is someone I can go to with a personal problem.
>
> My health benefits meet my family's needs.
>
> My pay relates well to my performance.

Strongly Agree	Agree	Neither Agree nor Disagree	Disagree	Strongly Disagree
5	4	3	2	1

Since scales have both a positive and a negative end, some surveys rotate them. They have some with the positive end on the right and others with the positive end on the left. The reasoning behind this strategy is that this makes the participant pay closer attention to wording and responses. Our experience has been that that approach leads to mistakes, and participants quite often mark the wrong points.

Another caution with scale response questions has to do with negative questions. A negative question often requires a positive scale response to be considered negative and a negative scale response to be considered positive. For example:

> Using the provided scale, indicate your agreement with the following statements:

> ❐ Job assignments in my department are made unfairly.

> ❐ The compensation program is administered unfairly.

> ❐ Vacations are required to be taken at times not preferred by employees.

Strongly Agree	Agree	Neither Agree nor Disagree	Disagree	Strongly Disagree
5	4	3	2	1

A Strongly Agree response is usually considered positive, but a Strongly Agree response to *these* three questions would be considered a negative opinion for tabulating survey results. A Strongly Disagree would be tabulated as a positive opinion.

Often these negative-type questions confuse the participants. They mark the reverse point of what they want. The tabulators can also be confused, so they must be made well aware of the desired responses. Otherwise, they may inadvertently tabulate and compile their responses in reverse.

Multiple-Choice Question Responses

Other multiple-choice questions might require other types of a scale for responses, such as:

Which of the following insurances is most important to you?

a. Health
b. Life
c. Dental
d. Disability
e. Prescription drugs

Depending on the question, you may also offer response alternatives such as None of the Above, All, and Other. Like the five-point scale responses, these can be marked on the survey or on a separate answer sheet.

Objective-Question Responses

In the examples, five possible responses were provided, so they could be answered on a five-response answer sheet. However, an objective question only allows for two or three responses:

Do you feel safe and secure in your work area?

1. Yes
2. No

Do our customers generally have a high opinion of our quality?

a. Yes
b. No
c. Don't know

Are you satisfied with the employee newsletter at your location?

a. Yes
b. No
c. Not applicable

If you are using a five-point answer sheet, you can assign the appropriate places for responses by number. You can use the first two or three positions and, for these questions, not use the other positions.

Types of Questions to Use

Our suggestion for written and online surveys is to use primarily multiple-choice questions that require five or fewer alternative responses. This will allow relatively easy tabulation and compiling of responses.

A final essay question can be of assistance. It provides a method for participants to supply any additional information not covered by the survey's multiple-choice questions. Fill-in questions and ranking questions should be used when there is not an alternative multiple-choice or objective question.

We prefer to use scale responses for the multiple-choice questions, and we try to use all five scales: satisfaction, importance, rating, amount, and agreement. Generally, we attempt to have a question for each dimension require a response from each scale.

An example of a five-point response answer sheet appears in Figure 7-1, but there are many versions of such answer sheets. They are available with a variety of question numbers and response options. Generally, they are furnished or specified by whoever is tabulating the survey results.

A separate answer sheet for fill-in, ranking, and essay responses can be used (described in detail in Chapter 8).

For online surveys, a similar format may be used. It can be adjusted as necessary and include fill-in, essay, and ranking questions.

Using these suggestions, you can develop guidelines for your survey and then create the questions.

Question Guidelines

The first guideline is to determine the number of questions for your survey. For that, you need to decide:

> How long should it take to complete the survey?
>
> How many demographic identification questions will you have?
>
> How many essay questions will you have?
>
> How many dimensions have you included?

Figure 7-1. Sample five-point response answer sheet.

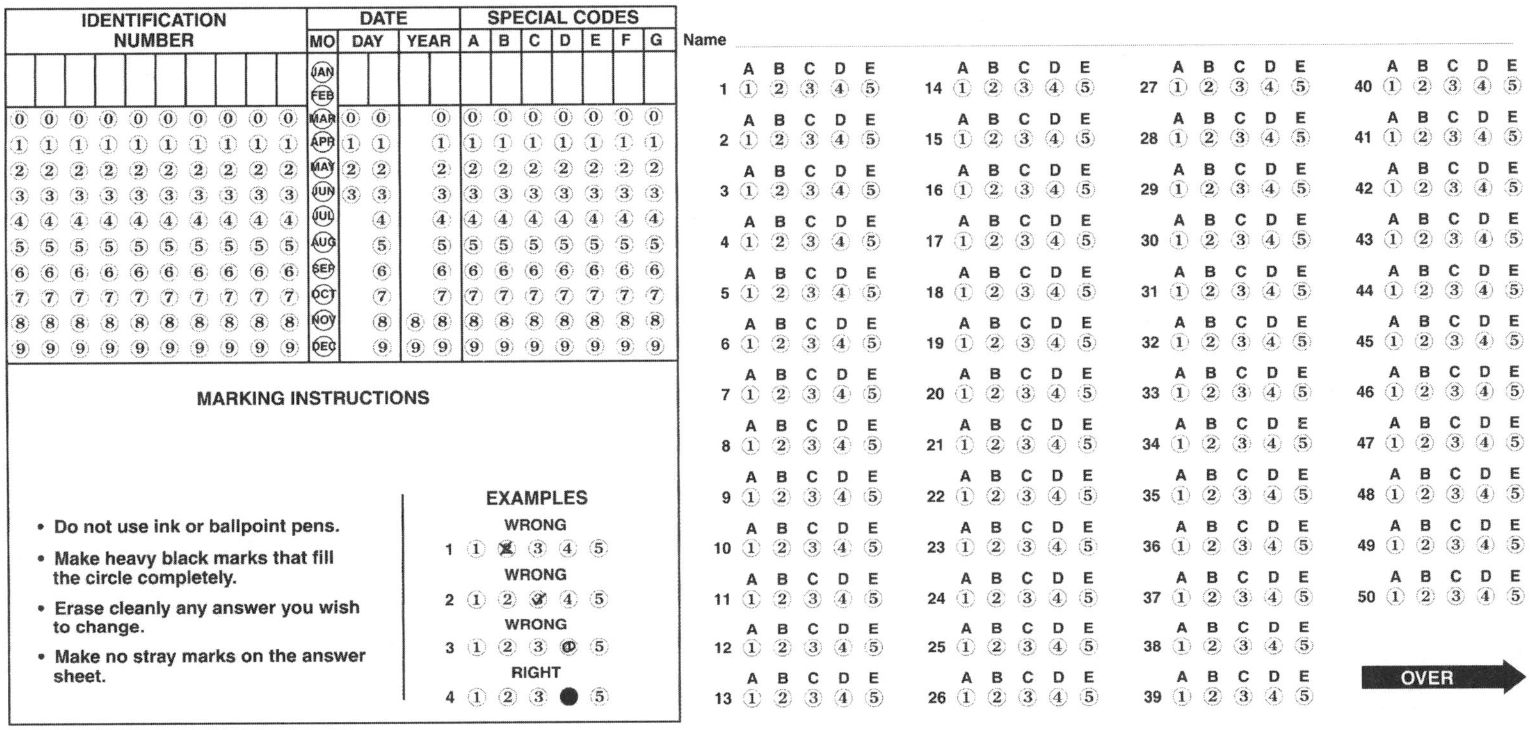

Figure 7-2. Determining question guidelines.

Desired time for completion of survey
_____ minutes x 60 =   a. _____ seconds

Number of demographic questions
_____ x 15 seconds =   b. _____ seconds

Number of essay questions
_____ x 120 seconds =   c. _____ seconds

Number of dimensions
_____ x 2 x 10 seconds =   d. _____ seconds

Total basic question time (b + c + d) =   e. _____ seconds

Available time for survey questions (a – e) =   f. _____ seconds

Total number of subareas in all areas   g. _____

Time per subarea (f ÷ g) =   h. _____ seconds

Questions per subarea (h ÷ 10) =   i. _____ questions

A Determining Question Guidelines form is shown in Figure 7-2. One is also provided on the accompanying disk.

If you have the information described above, you can complete the Determining Question Guidelines form. For example, assume your information was:

How long should it take to complete the survey? 50 minutes

How many demographic identification
questions will you have?   8

How many essay questions will you have?   1

How many dimensions have you included?   7

Your completed form would be similar to the one featured in Figure 7-3. Using that information, you have 37.4 available questions per dimension.

In some cases, you will have identified subareas of a dimension to survey. In those instances, you need to divide the number of questions for the dimension by the subareas identified for that dimension. That will give you a guideline for each subarea.

Using our example, you have 37.4 available questions per dimension.

Assume you identified the following subareas for the dimension of Compensation:

    Comparison with competitive companies

    Comparison of pay to job

    Comparison of pay to performance

    Company's compensation policy

    Bonus payment

    Basis for calculating bonus

There are six subareas, so using our earlier example of 37.4 questions for each dimension and dividing by 6 produces a guideline of six or seven questions for each subarea of Compensation.

Figure 7-3. Example of completed form for determining question guidelines.

Desired time for completion of survey
___50___ minutes x 60 =   a. ___3,000___ seconds

Number of demographic questions
___8___ x 15 seconds =   b. ___120___ seconds

Number of essay questions
___1___ x 120 seconds =   c. ___120___ seconds

Number of dimensions
___7___ x 2 x 10 seconds =   d. ___140___ seconds

Total basic question time (b + c + d) =   e. ___380___ seconds

Available time for survey questions (a – e) =   f. ___2,620___ seconds

Total number of dimensions   g. ___7___

Time per dimension (f ÷ g) =   h. ___347___ seconds

Questions per subarea (h ÷ 10) =   i. ___37.4 questions

Figure 7-4. Question development form.

Dimension _____ **Subarea** _____ **Question Guideline** _____

Specifics   **Questions**

_____   Satisfaction_____ Importance_____ Rating_____ Agreement_____
                          Other_____

_____   Satisfaction_____ Importance_____ Rating_____ Agreement_____
                          Other_____

_____   Satisfaction_____ Importance_____ Rating_____ Agreement_____
                          Other_____

_____   Satisfaction_____ Importance_____ Rating_____ Agreement_____
                          Other_____

_____   Satisfaction_____ Importance_____ Rating_____ Agreement_____
                          Other_____

_____   Satisfaction_____ Importance_____ Rating_____ Agreement_____
                          Other_____

_____   Satisfaction_____ Importance_____ Rating_____ Agreement_____
                          Other_____

_____   Satisfaction_____ Importance_____ Rating_____ Agreement_____
                          Other_____

_____   Satisfaction_____ Importance_____ Rating_____ Agreement_____
                          Other_____

_____   Satisfaction_____ Importance_____ Rating_____ Agreement_____
                          Other_____

Questions by Subareas

You have already identified the areas of each dimension you need to question, and you have a guideline as to the number of questions per dimension. Figure 7-4 features a Question Development Form. Like the other forms introduced in this book, it is on the accompanying disk.

The Question Development Form is to be used for each dimension subarea and for each dimension in which you did not identify a subarea to survey. You begin by completing the top of the form. For example, if the dimension is Facilities, the subarea is Environment, and the number of questions guideline is 6 (total per dimension divided by the number of subareas in the dimension), the completed top of the form would be:

Question Development Form

Dimension: Facilities_____
Subarea: Environment_____
Question Guideline: __6__

Next, you list the specifics of the subarea or dimension you wish to survey. For example, the following are several possible dimensions and one of their subareas. Each is followed by two specifics for which information could be sought:

Benefits/health insurance

❐ Cost to employee

❐ Enrollment period scheduling

Training and development/new procedures

❐ Availability

❐ Offered when required

Facilities/environment

❐ Amount of lighting

❐ Air quality

Staying with our example of completing a Question Development Form for Facilities/Environment, adding the specific could produce a form similar to:

Figure 7-5. Satisfaction questions.

Dimension _____ **Subarea** _____

Response Scale

| Very Satisfied | Somewhat Satisfied | Neither Satisfied nor Dissatisfied | Somewhat Dissatisfied | Very Dissatisfied |

Questions

How satisfied are you with _____?

How satisfied are you with _____?

How satisfied are you with _____?

How satisfied are you with _____?

How satisfied are you with _____?

How satisfied are you with _____?

How satisfied are you with _____?

How satisfied are you with _____?

How satisfied are you with _____?

How satisfied are you with _____?

How satisfied are you with _____?

How satisfied are you with _____?

How satisfied are you with _____?

How satisfied are you with _____?

How satisfied are you with _____?

Question Development Form

Dimension: Facilities _____
Subarea: Environment_____
Question Guideline:__6__

Specifics	Questions
Amount of Lighting	Satisfaction_____ Importance_____
	Rating_____Agreement_____
	Other_____

Each specific is followed by a line with the five scale alternatives: isfaction, importance, rating, amount, and agreement. There is also, the next line, other. After you have listed the subarea specifics fc dimension, check what you believe to be the appropriate question for or formats for each specific.

Earlier, the use of a question in each format for each dimension mentioned. A question in each format for each subarea can also attempted, but you do not have to use all question types. Select the q tion types that will obtain the type of information you are seeking.

You have to consider the number of questions guideline and within that number. On occasion, you may not use all available quest for an area. If that occurs, you can transfer some of those question another area.

If you must limit your questions and cannot use all five scale forn select the ones that you feel will best describe the information you de

If you wish to survey both satisfaction and importance for dimension and major subarea, you have to include those two questi

The Other category is provided when the scale formats will obtain the information you require. Here, you describe the type of c tion you need. For example, assume you want the participant to employee benefits in order of satisfaction, but a five-point scale doe provide for the fourteen benefits the questions offers. In such a case check Other and create the question with the type of response requ Sometimes, you might need to use a fill-in or essay question.

Once you have identified the type of questions, you can creat actual questions. Figures 7-5 through 7-9 consist of forms that c used. Each is for one type of question.

The scales on the forms can use either numbers or letters to in responses. You should use the format that corresponds with the a sheet you have elected to use. This will be detailed in Chapter 8.

(text continues on pa

Figure 7-6. Agreement questions.

Dimension _____**Subarea** _____

Response Scale

| Strongly Agree | Agree | Neither Agree nor Disagree | Disagree | Strongly Disagree |

Statements for Agreement/Disagreement

Figure 7-7. Rating questions.

Dimension _____ **Subarea** _____

Response Scale

Excellent   Very Good   Typical   Fair   Poor

Questions

How do you rate _____?

How do you rate _____?

How do you rate _____?

How do you rate _____?

How do you rate _____?

How do you rate _____?

How do you rate _____?

How do you rate _____?

How do you rate _____?

How do you rate _____?

How do you rate _____?

How do you rate _____?

How do you rate _____?

How do you rate _____?

How do you rate _____?

How do you rate _____?

How do you rate _____?

Figure 7-8. Amount questions.

Dimension _____**Subarea** _____

Response Scale

| Much Too Much | Too Much | Just Right | Too Little | Much Too Little |

Statements for Amount

Figure 7-9. Importance questions.

Dimension _____ **Subarea** _____

Response Scale

| Very Important | Somewhat Important | Neither Important nor Unimportant | Somewhat Unimportant | Very Unimportant |

Questions

How important to you is _____?

How important to you is _____?

How important to you is _____?

How important to you is _____?

How important to you is _____?

How important to you is _____?

How important to you is _____?

How important to you is _____?

How important to you is _____?

How important to you is _____?

How important to you is _____?

How important to you is _____?

How important to you is _____?

How important to you is _____?

How important to you is _____?

How important to you is _____?

You can complete a form for each dimension or subarea to be surveyed for each type of question you will be using.

Fill-In and Essay Question Development

At times, you may need to include fill-in questions. Generally, fill-in questions are limited to one or two words to ease the tabulation. We try to avoid using fill-in responses on written and online surveys unless there is a compelling reason. However, at times they are necessary.

> A New Hampshire company asked employees what one word best described their jobs.
>
> An Arizona company asked employees for the names of their supervisors.

If you are conducting an online survey, such question can be programmed into the flow and easily collected and displayed. They can also be collected by the interviewer and a focus group leader. When used with a written survey, space has to be provided on the answer sheet, or a separate answer sheet has to be provided for all written questions.

As mentioned earlier, a concluding essay question for additional comments is generally a good idea. It provides an opportunity for participants to explain any answers and add other information that can be of assistance.

Figure 7-10 features a form to note any supplemental questions you wish to include. It has four headings: Ranking Questions, Multiple-Choice Questions, Other, and Final Question.

The Ranking Questions section is for any question in which you want the participants to rank items. For example:

> Rank the following communications media with respect to their effectiveness. Write a 1 before the medium that you feel is most effective; a 2 in front of the next most effective; and so on.
>
> _____ Employee newsletter
>
> _____ Bulletin board
>
> _____ All employee meetings

Figure 7-10. Supplemental questions.

Ranking Questions

Multiple-Choice Questions

Other

Final Question

_____ E-mail

_____ Voice mail

_____ Department meetings

_____ Company-written memos to all employees

_____ Video messages

The Multiple-Choice Questions section is for questions whose responses do not work with the answer sheet. For example, assume your answer sheet allows for five possible responses, but you want to ask a multiple-choice question with eight possible responses. In that case, you can have the question on a supplemental answer sheet.

The Other section is for any additional questions you wish to ask that do not fit any of the other categories.

The Final Question section is to identify a concluding question such as:

> Do you have any additional information that you feel will assist this employee opinion survey in meeting its objective? If so, write it in the space below.

Conclusion

With the forms introduced in this chapter, you are ready to construct the survey instrument.

CHAPTER 8

CREATING THE SURVEY INSTRUMENT

To spell out the obvious is often to call it in question.

ERIC HOFFER,
The Passionate State of Mind

You have the dimensions and subareas determined along with their questions. You have identified the demographic information you require. It is now time to actually construct the survey instrument. Regardless of whether you are using a written or online format, you still need to construct the instrument. Both formats have the same elements:

> Introduction
>
> Instructions
>
> Survey questions
>
> Submission

Introduction

Even if you plan on having the introduction and instructions given orally by an administrator, you should have a written introduction as part of the instrument. That introduction should describe:

> The purpose/objective of the survey
>
> A report of survey results
>
> The use of survey results
>
> The confidentiality of survey responses
>
> How to ask questions

Purpose/Objective of the Survey

This should be a clear statement of the reason for conducting the survey. It should be the one developed as the first step in preparing for the survey, but written in a manner for the survey participants. For example:

> You are about to participate in a survey designed to collect the opinions of our employees regarding the conditions of employment at our company. This is the second such survey that has been conducted. The first was conducted two years ago, and the information produced proved to be of assistance in making our company an even better place at which to work. We have every hope this survey will be of equal assistance.

Sometimes, a letter from the chief executive of the company or unit to be surveyed is used. When it is, it is generally produced on company letterhead and signed.

Report of Survey Results

Our recommendation is that the results of a survey should always be reported to those who participate in it. For example:

We will have the results of the survey within two months. At that time, employee meetings will be held to share those results, answer your questions, and describe management's plans.

Use of Survey Results

However they are to be used, survey results should be communicated. A detailed description of the process is not necessary—just the broad outlines. For example:

If the initial results of the survey indicate additional information is required, focus groups will be conducted with a random selection of employees and the information from those meetings included in a final survey report.

Then meetings will be held with all employees to communicate the survey results and provide an opportunity for questions. Those meetings will be followed by department meetings to review survey results that apply to your work areas and to develop plans for continual improvement.

As with past surveys, we view this as an opportunity to continue and improve our two-way communication process that has proved so effective.

Confidentiality of Survey Responses

This should describe the confidentiality of the responses and also the use of demographic information.

Your responses are completed anonymously. There is a place to enter your name, but that is not required. In addition, some other demographic information is requested. It is information that allows results to be reported in terms of different groups.

By being able to report the results broken down by these various groupings, such as department and length of service, it provides us all with more usable information.

If you are uncomfortable supplying demographic data, you may leave some or all of those areas blank, but it is hoped you will see their value and supply the requested responses.

How to Ask Questions

Whatever format is being used, a method to ask procedural questions should be provided. In a group- or individually administered survey, it could be:

> If you have any questions regarding the survey's purpose, use, and confidentiality, ask the person administering the survey.

For a written survey mailed to the participants or an online survey being completed away from an administrator, it could be:

> If you have any questions regarding the survey's purpose, use, and confidentiality, you can call (name) at (telephone number) between (times).

For online surveys, you can also provide an e-mail address, but that may require the participant to wait for a reply before continuing.

Instructions

Once the introduction is completed and any participant questions answered, the specific completion instructions are next. Even if you plan on having the introduction and instructions given orally by an administrator, you should have written instructions as part of the instrument. Those instructions should describe:

> The introduction of the survey instrument
>
> How to respond to the survey questions
>
> How to use your code or password
>
> How to ask questions

Introduction of the Survey Instrument

The participant now needs instructions in how to complete the survey, and the first item is to describe the actual survey instrument—the format. If using an online survey, the screen might display this:

Our employee opinion survey is offered online. Each of its questions appears on a separate screen along with alternative answers from which to select or space for you to write an answer. Each screen indicates how to answer the question on that screen. When you have completed your answer, press Enter on your keyboard or left click Continue with the mouse. That will record your response and display the next question.

Typically, online surveys do not offer the option of returning to a previous question. Whatever the case, your instructions should so state. For example, if a participant cannot go back you might say:

Once you have moved to the next question, you may not return to the previous question, so you must answer a question at the time it is displayed.

If the participant can go back:

Anytime during the survey, you may return to a previous question and change your response. To do so, press the Insert key on your keyboard or left click Back with your mouse.

With a written survey, you need to describe the question and answer formats. Assuming you will be using a booklet of questions, a separate multiple-choice answer sheet, and a separate written response sheet, your introduction to them could be similar to:

Our survey instrument consists of three parts: a survey booklet and two answer sheets.

The survey booklet contains all of our survey questions, but you do not record your answers in it. Instead, you read the question and then respond on the appropriate sheet.

One of the answer sheets is for responding to the multiple-choice questions. It is the one with the (squares or circles) to be darkened. The multiple-choice questions are the first ones in the survey.

The second answer sheet is for responding to those questions that request written answers. Those questions are the last ones in the survey.

It is important that the participants understand the instrument before communicating how to complete it, so whatever format is being used, a similar question resolution statement can appear here.

> If you have any questions regarding the survey's purpose, use, and confidentiality, ask the person administering the survey.

For a written survey mailed to the participants or an online survey being completed away from an administrator, it could be:

> If you have any questions regarding the survey's purpose, use, and confidentiality, you can call (name) at (telephone number) between (times).

How to Respond to Survey Questions

You are now ready to provide specific instructions in how to respond to the survey questions. The instructions will vary by survey format and method of administration. For online surveys, the instructions usually appear on each screen. For example, a multiple-choice question might appear as:

How do you rate the quality of the formal communication you receive from the company?

Left click on one of the following to indicate your answer:
Excellent   Very Good   Good   Fair   Poor

A fill-in question might appear as:

What single word best describes our company?

Type your answer on the following line:

_____

Instructions for a written survey appear at the beginning of the survey document and could be similar to:

> The majority of this survey consists of questions and statements with five possible responses. You should read each and then choose the response that best represents your opinion.
>
> At times, you may not feel any of the responses for a question fully describes your opinion. If that occurs, select the response that most closely fits your opinion. Try not to leave a question without a response.
>
> There are no right or wrong answers to these questions. They ask for your opinion—what you think—so whatever your opinion is, that is the correct response.
>
> Your responses are to be marked on the separate answer sheet. The answer sheet contains numbers that match the question numbers in the survey booklet. Each number is followed by five small (squares or circles). Each of the (squares or circles) is in a column that is headed by a (letter or number) that matches the responses offered in the survey booklet.
>
> Locate the correct response for the question, and then darken the (square or circle). Darken it completely using the pencil provided. Do not use any other marking instrument. The answer sheets are machine-tabulated, and marking instruments such as pens are not recognized by the machine.
>
> If you wish to change an answer, completely erase the first one and then mark the new one.
>
> Remember, mark only one response for each question. If you mark more than one, your responses to that question will not be tabulated.

Most answer sheets have one or two practice response areas. If so, the instructions should lead the participants through completion of those responses.

> For the final questions in the survey, use the second answer sheet. In fact, those questions are actually printed on that answer sheet. The survey booklet will direct you to its use.

If you have any questions regarding the survey's purpose, use, and confidentiality, ask the person administering the survey.

For a written survey mailed to the participants or an online survey being completed away from an administrator, it could be:

> If you have any questions regarding the survey's purpose, use, and confidentiality, you can call (name) at (telephone number) between (times).

How to Use Your Code or Password

If you are using a code or password for online surveys, you can enter it at this point in order to access the survey questions. However, some online surveys require the password at the very beginning—before even the introduction is displayed.

Wherever it is required, the screen should contain instructions of how to enter it and solutions if problems are encountered. You can also include a reaffirmation that the password is completely random and cannot be identified with the individual employee using it.

If you are using two answer sheets with a written survey, you need to cross-reference them. The first sheet will have demographic information, and you want to be able to relate that information to any responses on the second sheet. One method of accomplishing this is to say something like:

> You will note on your first answer sheet a space for a six-character ID. The purpose of using an identification number is to coordinate your two answer sheets, and that allows reporting by the various demographic groupings.
>
> So, make up a six-character ID. It can be all numbers, all letters, or a combination of numbers and letters. Then write that ID in the identification space. Now, write that same ID on the second answer sheet where required.

Note that, in some cases, you may want the participant to record the number by darkening appropriate squares or circles. If so, your instructions will have to comply with the specific requirement of the answer sheet you are using.

How to Ask Questions

You have now completed all instructions, and even though you have provided opportunities throughout the instructions for questions, you need to do so one last time:

> If you have any questions regarding the survey's purpose, use, and confidentiality, ask the person administering the survey.

For a written survey mailed to the participants or an online survey being completed away from an administrator, this statement could be:

> If you have any questions regarding the survey's purpose, use, and confidentiality, you can call (name) at (telephone number) between (times).

Survey Questions

You are now ready to construct the survey questions. You have already identified the demographics, dimensions, subareas, number of questions, and types of questions, so you will need those completed forms.

Demographics

The lead-in for the demographics page is similar to this:

> Our survey results can be made more meaningful by grouping them by types of employees as well as reporting for all employees. For that reason, the following demographic information is being requested. It is not information that can be used to identify individual employees, but if you do not feel comfortable supplying any or all of this information, leave those questions blank.
>
> Each of the following questions requires only one response. Read the question and then make the appropriate response.

You then list your demographic questions. We normally present them in the following order—leaving out those not required:

Department

Employee classification

Length of service

Gender

Race

Age

Any other areas

In a written survey, try to have all demographic questions on the first pages of the survey. Then begin the actual survey questions on a new page.

Dimension Questions

You have already identified the questions you wish to ask and their number and type (importance, satisfaction, amount, rating, and agreement). They can be presented in four basic formats:

Grouped by dimension but mixed

Grouped by dimension and then by type

Grouped by type but mixed

Grouped by type and then by dimension

There are some surveys that offer questions in groupings by dimension and mix types of questions within each grouping. We have found more consistent results when questions are grouped by type and then by dimension subarea within each type and the types are then sequenced as follows:

Importance

Agreement

Amount

Rating

Satisfaction

You do not have to use all types for each survey. When you have fewer types, you can still use the same sequence without the type excluded.

The importance questions for the dimensions (not the subareas) are often listed separately as the first item. The same can be done with the satisfaction questions for the dimensions, but they can be listed as the last item.

The order for the questions within a type can be based on their importance to the survey or just random. Generally, benefit questions follow compensation questions, and training and development questions are located by career opportunity questions.

For written questions, begin each page with instructions and the scale for the type of questions on the page. If you change types in midpage, begin the new type with instructions and scale.

For online surveys, begin a series of screens for a question type with instructions and the scale. These are then repeated on each screen in that series.

Written Questions

For written surveys, the questions that require ranking, multiple choice with more responses than provided on an answer sheet, fill-ins, and essay questions are typically provided on a separate sheet with space for answers and are the last questions in the survey.

Submission

The final element of the survey is instructions on how to submit it when completed. For an online survey, this is generally to just hit the final Enter on the keyboard or to left mouse click on Submit.

For written surveys that are mailed, use instructions such as:

When you have completed your survey, place the question booklet and answer sheets into the accompanying self-addressed, stamped envelope and mail. If you lose the envelope, you may mail the survey to:

(Appropriate name and address)

Completed surveys must be received no later than (date) to be included in the tabulation.

For a written survey that is administered to a group:

When you have completed your survey, place the survey booklet on the table by the exit. Deposit your answer sheets in the box by the exit.

For written surveys individually completed:

When you have completed your survey return the survey booklet to the person who gave it to you and deposit your answer sheets in the box (location).

Sometimes with individually administered written surveys, you can have the participant place it in an addressed, stamped envelope and deposit it in an outgoing mailbox in the area.

Answer Sheets

Several times we have referred to answer sheets that are preprinted for scanning and computer tabulation. These answer sheets must be obtained in advance from whoever will be doing such tabulation. The guidelines you can consider for selecting answer sheets are:

Ensure there are enough response categories for the number of questions on your survey.

Ensure the number of responses per question agrees with the responses offered.

Ensure there is some form of identification space.

Ensure practice question responses are numbered or lettered separately from the other questions.

Ensure, if possible, that the demographic questions' responses are separate on the sheet with different identifications—for example, alphabetical instead of numerical.

A Complete Survey

The next chapter consists of a complete employee opinion survey.

CHAPTER 9

A SAMPLE EMPLOYEE OPINION SURVEY

People don't care how much you know, until they know how much you care ...

ZIG ZIGLAR,
Top Performance

The employee opinion survey that follows was created and used by a small New England HMO and was one of a series of annual surveys. Because the survey is presented as written by the company, some of the terms used are specific to that company. It is provided so you can review a relatively simple but complete survey that was actually used by a company.

Accompanying the survey are copies of the two answer sheets. Also included is an instruction letter that was used with surveys mailed to those who could not attend.

Although this survey is for a specific company, many of its questions and other wording may be of assistance to you. Although some may have been covered as samples in earlier chapters, the survey is also reproduced on the accompanying disk for copying and revision.

An Annual Employee Opinion Survey

(Company Letterhead)
(Date)

To all employees:

You are about to participate in an employee opinion survey. We conduct such a survey every year to provide an opportunity for you to communicate your opinions about the conditions of employment at our company. All employees will have an opportunity to complete a survey, and some will also be invited to participate in small groups to provide any needed additional information.

We will have the results of the survey within two months. At that time, an all-employee meeting will be held to review those results. That meeting will be followed by department meetings in which you can raise questions and develop suggestions for contributing to our company's conditions of employment.

Your responses to the survey questions will be held in confidence. You will not be asked to identify yourself. For those who wish to do so, a place is provided at the end of the survey, but that is optional. You are not required or expected to give your name.

The completed surveys will be collected by representatives of our employee opinion survey consulting firm. They will tabulate and report the results. They will be the only ones to actually see the completed surveys.

As with past surveys, you will be asked to provide some personal information. Such information allows the results to be reported by different groupings of employees such as department and length of service.

If you are uncomfortable supplying that type of data, you may leave those questions blank, but it is hoped you will see their value and supply the requested responses.

We view our annual employee opinion surveys as an opportunity to continue to improve the two-way communication process at our company.

Thank you for your participation,
(Signature and Title)

Instructions

Our survey consists of three items: this booklet, which contains all of our survey questions, and two answer sheets. You are not to write in this booklet. All your answers are to be on the two answer sheets.

The first answer sheet is for the majority of the survey questions. Each question is followed by several possible responses. When you select your response, you mark it on the answer sheet after the number of the question.

The second answer sheet is for responses that cannot be recorded on the first answer sheet. These are the last questions of the survey.

Use a number 2 pencil to mark all your answers. The answer sheets are machine-tabulated, and only number 2 pencil marks are recognized by the machine.

The first step is to code the two answer sheets. You are going to write the same number on both sheets. This is not to identify you. It is to ensure your responses on the two answer sheets are tabulated together.

Note: at the top left section of the first answer sheet is a heading—Identification Number. Beneath it are ten small boxes.

Using the first seven small boxes, write a seven-digit number with one number in each small box. It can be any seven digits you wish.

Identification Number

  1 0 1 9 2 0 4 _ _ _

The last three small boxes are to be used to identify your department. This will allow the survey to be tabulated by department and the results reported to each department. From the following list, find the three-digit number that identifies your department and write it in the last three small boxes.

Finance

101 Finance

102 Information Services

103 Other Finance

Health Services

201 Provider Relations/Wellness

202 Health Care Management

203 Medical, Quality, and Risk Management

204 Utilization Review

205 Other Health Services

Administration

301 Claims/COB

302 Group Administration/Billing

303 Office Services/Claims Control

304 Other Administration

Marketing

401 Member Services

402 Sales and Service

403 Other Marketing

All Other Departments

500 All Other Departments

For example, using the earlier same seven digits and assuming your are in the Member Services department, your final number would be:

Identification Number

1 0 1 9 2 0 4 4 0 1

The second answer sheet also has space at the top for a ten-digit number. Write in that space the same number your just wrote on the first answer sheet.

Your two answer sheets should now have the same ten-digit number at the top.

Now, return to your first answer sheet. Note that beneath each of the numbers you entered is a column of small circles. They are identified as zero through nine. Since our tabulating equipment cannot read handwriting, we need to code the identification number you just created. To do this, find the appropriate circle beneath each digit and darken it. For example, using the number shown earlier, the coding would appear as:

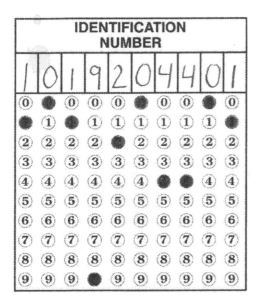

The next area on the first answer sheet is headed Date. Then there is a Month, Day, and Year subheading. The subheadings have columns of circles beneath them. First, in the Month column, darken the circle for this month.

Next, in the Day column, darken the circle or circles for today's date. Finally, in the Year column, darken the circle for the last digit of this year.

If today was July 14, 2002, your answer sheet would appear as:

The next area is headed Special Codes, and beneath it are seven small boxes each headed by a letter (A through G). We are going to use these for recording demographic information. This is the information that will allow results to be reported by various employee groupings. However, if you are uncomfortable answering them, leave them blank and turn to the next page.

Read the following questions, then select your answer to each question, and record it in the box headed by the same letter as the question by darkening the appropriate circle in the column beneath each small box.

A. What is your length of service with our company?
1. Six months or less
2. From six months to one year
3. From one year to three years
4. From three years to five years
5. More than five years

B. Of which group of employees are you?
1. Executive

2. Management
3. Supervisor
4. Professional
5. Clerical
6. Other

C. Of which group are you?
1. Caucasian
2. African-American
3. Hispanic
4. Native American
5. Asian
6. Other

D. What is your gender?
1. Male
2. Female

Your answer sheets are now prepared, and you are ready to begin the survey. Here are a few final instructions:

If you need to change an answer, fully erase the old answer and then mark your new one.

There are five possible responses provided for each question, but you only mark one response for each question.

There are no right or wrong answers. You are being asked to share your opinions, and whatever your opinion is is the correct response.

Select the best alternative response from those given—the one that closest reflects your opinion. If no choices exactly fit your opinion, try to select the one that comes closest. However, if none of the responses reflects your opinion, you can leave the question blank.

As you are answering the questions in this survey, you may wish to provide additional information or explain an answer. If so, space is provided on the second answer sheet.

You may have all the time necessary to complete the survey. When completed, place your answer sheets in the box by the door and your survey booklet on the table by the door.

If you have to leave the room during the survey, leave all your materials on the desk until you return.

If you have any questions, ask the administrator.

Questions

On this page, the survey questions begin. Note they are each identified here and on the answer sheet by a number. Be sure to mark your response after the appropriate number on the answer sheet.

Each of the following questions requests you to indicate how important to you various conditions of employment at our company are. Indicate your response using the following scale. Be sure to darken the appropriate lettered box.

Very Important	Important	Neither Important nor Unimportant	Unimportant	Very Unimportant
A	B	C	D	E

1. How important to you is it to work at our company?

2. How important to you are employee policies at the company for which you work?

3. How important to you is the consistent administration of company policies?

4. How important is the work you do to our company's success?

5. How important to you is the job you do?

6. How important to you is the fairness of the way your company treats all employees?

7. How important to you is the overall training and development provided by your company?

8. How important to you is job security?

9. How important to you is the type of supervision you receive?

10. How important to you is it to be involved in quality customer service?

11. How important to you is the way your company deals with change?

12. How important to you is the overall communication at your company?

13. How important to you is the salary you receive?

14. How important to you is your total cash compensation?

15. How important to you are the benefits you receive?

16. How important to you are the overall operating procedures of the department in which you work?

17. How important to you are the opportunities to advance at our company?

18. How important to you is the performance of executive management?

19. How important to you is the quality of customer service provided by your company?

20. How important to you is the recognition you receive from your company?

How important are each of the benefits provided by our company?

21. Vision Benefits

22. Eyeglasses Discount

23. Employee Life Insurance

24. Dependant Life Insurance

25. Additional Employee Life Insurance

26. Employee Referral Plan

27. Accidental Death and Dismemberment Insurance

28. Travel Insurance

29. Time Away from Work

30. Employee Dental Insurance

31. Dependant Dental Insurance

32. Flexible Work Hours

33. Employee Health Care Coverage

34. Dependant Health Care Coverage

35. Pension Plan

36. Gainsharing

37. Tuition Reimbursement

38. Short-Term Disability Insurance

39. Long-Term Disability Insurance

40. Employee Assistance Plan

41. Prescription Drug Plan

The next statements are concerning your job and our company. Indicate the extent to which you personally agree or disagree with each one using the following scale for your responses:

Strongly Agree	Agree	Neither Agree nor Disagree	Disagree	Strongly Disagree
A	B	C	D	E

42. I am proud to work for our company.

43. Company employee policies are administered the same in all departments.

44. I like my job—the work I do.

45. I am satisfied with the training provided for my current job.

46. I am satisfied with the amount of training offered for advancement.

47. Our company is concerned with the long-term welfare of its employees.

48. I feel secure that I will be able to work for our company as long as I do a good job.

49. I feel I can voice my opinion without fear of reprisal.

50. My supervisor is technically competent.

51. My supervisor is competent in human relations.

52. My supervisor deals with all employees fairly.

53. My supervisor deals with employee problems fairly.

54. Our company handles change well.

55. The communication I receive from the company is accurate.

56. The communication I receive from the company is timely.

57. Our company maintains salary levels that compare well to other companies in the area.

58. Our new incentive program is part of my total cash compensation.

59. Our company maintains benefits that compare well to other companies in the area.

60. I receive cooperation from other departments.

61. My department is well organized for the work it does.

62. The employees in my department work well as a team.

63. Company employee policies are properly and equally administered in my department.

64. I feel there is adequate opportunity for me to move to a better job within our company.

65. The job posting policy and procedure supports the advancement opportunities at our company.

66. My supervisor is concerned with providing quality service.

67. The employees of other departments are concerned with quality customer service.

68. Other departments are concerned with providing quality service.

69. I feel executive management is committed to quality customer service.

70. The company's executive management is concerned with providing quality service.

71. My supervisor recognizes my performance.

72. I have an annual set of performance standards.

73. Our company recognizes the accomplishments of employees.

74. I receive regular performance reviews.

On this page and the next one are questions to be answered using the following rating scale:

Excellent	Very Good	Typical	Fair	Poor
A	B	C	D	E

75. How do you rate our company as a place to work compared with other companies you know about?

76. How do you rate our company on treating employee problems fairly?

77. How do you rate the overall relationship between the company and its employees?

78. All things considered, how do you rate our company?

79. How do the company's employee policies compare with those of other companies you know about?

80. All things considered, how do you rate our company's employee policies and procedures?

81. All things considered, how do you like your job?

82. All things considered, how do you rate the fairness with which our company treats all employees?

83. All things considered, how do you rate the overall training and development provided?

84. How do you rate our company's business prospects for the next five years?

85. All things considered, how do you rate the job security provided by our company?

86. How do you rate your supervisor's credibility?

87. All things considered, how do you rate the supervision you receive?

88. All things considered, how do you rate the way in which our company deals with change as it relates to your job?

89. How do you rate the amount of communication you receive from our company?

90. How do you rate the level of communication of employee policies and procedures?

91. How do you rate the amount of communication you receive regarding quality customer service?

92. How do you rate the amount of communication you receive regarding the company's plans?

93. How do you rate the amount of communication you receive regarding reorganization?

94. All things considered, how do you rate the overall communication at our company?

95. How do you rate the total cash compensation you receive compared to what you could receive for similar work from another company in the area?

96. How do you rate the relationship between the amount of compensation you receive and your performance?

97. All things considered, how do you rate our company's overall total cash compensation program?

98. How do you rate the benefits you receive compared to those you could receive from another company in the area?

99. All things considered, how do you rate our company's overall benefits?

100. In your opinion, how do employees of other departments rate your department?

101. All things considered, how do you rate your department's overall operating procedures?

102. How do you rate your long-term career potential at our company?

103. All things considered, how do you rate the opportunities to advance at our company?

104. How do you rate the credibility of our executive management?

105. All things considered, how do you rate executive management's performance?

106. All things considered, how do you rate the quality of our customer service?

107. All things considered, how do you rate the recognition you receive at our company?

On this page are questions to be answered using the following scale:

Much Too Much	Too Much	Just Right	Too Little	Much Too Little
A	B	C	D	E

108. How do you feel about the quantity of work you are asked to perform?

109. How do you feel about the quality of work you are asked to perform?

110. How do you feel about the amount of time your supervisor spends with you?

111. How do you feel about the amount of change occurring within our company?

112. How do you feel about the amount of organizational change as it relates to our company?

113. How do you feel about the amount of organizational change as it relates to quality customer service?

114. How do you feel about the number of approvals required to get a decision made?

115. How much concern do you feel our company's executive management has for our company members?

116. How much concern do you feel our company's executive management has for our providers?

117. How much concern do you feel our company's executive management has for our employees?

118. How much concern do you feel our company's executive management has for customers?

119. How much has the quality of our company's customer service changed over the last year?

120. What is your level of understanding of quality customer service?

On this page are questions to be answered using the following scale:

Very Satisfied	*Satisfied*	*Neither Satisfied nor Dissatisfied*	*Dissatisfied*	*Very Dissatisfied*
A	B	C	D	E

121. All things considered, how satisfied are you with our company?

122. All things considered, how satisfied are you with our company's employee policies?

123. All things considered, how satisfied are you with your job?

124. All things considered, how satisfied are you with the fairness of the way the company treats all employees?

125. All things considered, how satisfied are you with the training and development provided by our company?

126. All things considered, how satisfied are you with your job security at our company?

127. All things considered, how satisfied are you with the supervision you receive?

128. All things considered, how satisfied are you with your level of involvement in quality customer service?

129. All things considered, how satisfied are you with the way our company deals with change as it relates to your job?

130. All things considered, how satisfied are you with the overall communication at our company?

131. All things considered, how satisfied are you with your salary at our company?

132. All things considered, how satisfied are you with the benefits provided by our company?

133. All things considered, how satisfied are you with your department's overall operating procedures?

134. All things considered, how satisfied are you with the opportunities to advance at our company?

135. All things considered, how satisfied are you with the company's quality standards?

136. All things considered, how satisfied are you with the changes that have been made to the quality standards?

137. All things considered, how satisfied are you with the quality of customer service?

138. How satisfied are you with the amount of change occurring within our company?

139. How satisfied are you with the amount of organizational change as it relates to our company?

140. How satisfied are you with the amount of organizational change as it relates to quality customer service?

141. All things considered, how satisfied are you with the recognition you receive at our company?

Rate your satisfaction with each of the benefits provided by our company.

142. Vision Benefits

143. Eyeglasses Discount

144. Employee Life Insurance

145. Dependant Life Insurance

146. Additional Employee Life Insurance

147. Employee Referral Plan

148. Accidental Death and Dismemberment Insurance

149. Travel Insurance

150. Time Away from Work

151. Employee Dental Insurance

152. Dependant Dental Insurance

153. Flexible Work Hours

154. Employee Health Care Coverage

155. Dependant Health Care Coverage

156. Pension Plan

157. Gainsharing

158. Tuition Reimbursement

159. Short-Term Disability Insurance

160. Long-Term Disability Insurance

161. Employee Assistance Plan

162. Prescription Drug Plan

For the following question, use the answers shown and respond by darkening the appropriate letter.

163. From what source do you receive most of your information about our company and your job?

163. A   Grapevine

163. B   Supervisor

163. C   Other employees

163. D   Company publications

163. E   Meetings

163. F   Bulletin boards

163. G   Newsletter

163. H   Other

Supplemental Answer Sheet

Identification Number

— — — — — — — — — —

164. If you have any additional information or comments that you feel will be of assistance to this survey, please write them in the space below.

Conclusion

This chapter included a set of materials actually used in a company's employee opinion survey process. It provides an opportunity to review the approach and documents one company used, but it is not presented as the correct approach for another company.

Each survey should reflect the identified conditions within a specific company. Likewise, any accompanying communication should be based on the company's history with such surveys and the methods in which the survey will be administered.

The next chapter deals with the administration of the survey.

PART THREE

CONDUCTING YOUR EMPLOYEE OPINION SURVEY

CHAPTER 10

ADMINISTERING
THE SURVEY

*Even in slight things the experience of the new is rarely
without some stirring or foreboding.*

ERIC HOFFER,
The Ordeal of Change

Once you have your survey preparations completed, you are
ready to implement the survey. One of the key decisions made
was who was to actually administer the survey. Whoever that is—
internal employees, external personnel, or a combination of
both—they need to become familiar with the survey instrument
and the administration rules and instructions you have established.

Administrator Training

Whatever format you have selected—focus group, interview,
written, or online—someone has to provide the participant with

the survey and answer any procedural questions. Even when the survey is done completely by computer or mail, someone has to be available for questions.

If an external firm is conducting the survey with its personnel, you probably only need to orient the people to your company's facilities, attendance procedures, and administration rules. If you are using your employees or people not experienced with survey administration, you need to conduct a training program. There are some exceptions: Focus groups and interviews require experienced people, people already well trained in their procedures, so you will probably not be conducting any additional training for them. Also, mailed surveys will not require special training for the people implementing them.

However, anyone administering a survey in a written or online format needs to know:

> The company's objective in conducting the survey
>
> The confidentiality of survey information
>
> The dates of any past surveys
>
> Any particular problems associated with past surveys
>
> The facility, equipment, and supplies required for the survey and arrangements for them
>
> When and how survey feedback will be given to employees
>
> Who will be available to answer any questions or problems
>
> Security procedures
>
> The mechanics of the survey (forms, answer sheets, etc.)
>
> What to say regarding the instructions for the survey and that they are responsible for distributing the survey

If it is necessary to actually train the administrators versus just orienting them, an effective approach is to have them actually participate in the survey. Then you can review with them the rules and instructions and answer any questions they have. You also need to describe the facility arrangements, schedules, and required supplies for the survey. Typically, such training requires an hour plus the time necessary to complete the survey.

Administration Guide

Each administrator should receive an administration guide that contains the information required to successfully execute the survey. It should include:

> A schedule
>
> A checklist of equipment and supplies
>
> The instructions
>
> The name and telephone number of someone to call for assistance

Schedule

The schedule should indicate not only the administrator's schedule but also the employees' schedules—who or how many employees are scheduled at what times—and who to contact if a scheduled employee does not arrive to participate in the survey.

Along with the schedules should be a description of the security device being used to ensure an employee is eligible to participate and can only participate once. Also, the administrator needs to know what to do if an employee arrives to participate at other than her scheduled time. If it is not an issue of pay and the employee can be accommodated, it is probably best to allow the employee to participate at that time.

A Maryland-based utility conducted its written survey by groups. The administrator was an external consultant, but an employee of the company's human resources department attended each session.

The human resources employee was assigned to check each employee, so there would be a record of who took the survey and who did not as well as ensuring no one took it more than once. (The surveys themselves were anonymous.)

After the first group (there were to be eight such groups), several employees approached the consultant to complain about the presence of the human resources person. They felt it was a violation of the pledge of anonymity.

Even though the human resources person could not tell who completed which survey, the person was moved to outside of the room to check people as they entered.

There must have been a reason the employees were so suspicious, but the point is that the presence of the internal person had the potential of affecting responses.

The administrator should be available before scheduled survey times to check facilities and supplies and, if an online survey is being used, to turn on computers. This will allow any problems to be identified and corrected in advance.

Checklist for Supplies and Equipment

A checklist for the administrator provides a method of ensuring all is in order before the participants begin the survey.

For written surveys administered to groups, the checklist should cover:

The room set-up

Pencils or other marking devices

A pencil sharpener, if needed

Enough surveys and answer sheets for all participants

Envelopes and/or drop box

For written surveys administered to individuals:

A private room or cubicle for completion

Pencils or other marking devices

A pencil sharpener, if needed

Enough surveys and answer sheets for all participants

Envelopes and/or drop box

For online surveys

Computers
Loaded and accessible surveys

Instructions

Individually administered mailed written surveys and online surveys should include the instructions. The administrator only needs to be available for questions. However, group-administered written surveys require the administrator to provide instructions.

The following instructions are written for the administrator of a group-administered survey. The italicized words are a suggested script. These instructions are on the disk accompanying this book and may be used by you as is or revised to meet your specific requirements.

A Suggested Guide

Once all participants have arrived, welcome them and then review the instructions for the survey. If the survey includes a letter or other communication from an executive of the company, read it to the employees. You may start by saying:

You are about to participate in a survey designed to collect the opinions of our employees regarding the conditions of employment at our company.

Tell them if this is the first survey or one of a series of surveys that is regularly conducted. If one of a series, tell them when the last one was conducted and how the results were used.

The results from this survey will be available in approximately (fill in the time).

If the initial results of the survey indicate additional information is required, focus groups with randomly selected employees will be

You answer by darkening the appropriate circle. Use the number two pencil we have provided. Do not use anything else, such as a pen, since the machine that tabulates the results will not recognize anything but a number 2 pencil.

The second answer sheet is for responding to those questions that request written answers. Those questions are the last ones in the survey.

The instructions for recording responses will vary by survey format. The following can be used as a guideline:

The majority of this survey consists of questions and statements with five possible responses. You should read each question and then decide what you believe to be the response that best represents your opinion.

At times, you may not feel that any of the responses for a question fully describes your opinion. If that occurs, select the response closest to your opinion. Try not to leave a question without a response.

There are no right or wrong answers to these questions. They ask for your opinion—what you think—so whatever your opinion is, that is the correct response.

Your responses are marked on a separate answer sheet. The answer sheet contains numbers that agree with the question numbers in the survey booklet. Each is followed by five small (squares or circles). Each of the (squares or circles) is in a column that is headed by a (letter or number) that equates with the responses offered in the survey booklet.

Locate the correct response for the question, and then darken the (square or circle). Darken it completely using the pencil provided. Do not use any other marking instrument. The answer sheets are machine-tabulated and marking instruments such as pens are not recognized by the machine.

If you wish to change an answer, completely erase the first one and then mark the new one.

Remember, you mark only one response for each question. If you mark more than one, your responses to that question will not be tabulated.

Most answer sheets have one or two practice response areas. If so, lead the participants through completion of those responses. Then check for questions.

The final questions in the survey use a second answer sheet. In fact, those questions are actually printed on that answer sheet. The survey booklet will direct you to its use.

If you are using two answer sheets, you need to cross-reference them. The first sheet will have demographic information, and you want to be able to relate that information to any responses on the second sheet. One method of accomplishing this is to say to participants:

You will note on your first answer sheet a space for a seven-digit identification number. The purpose of using an identification number is to coordinate your two answer sheets, which allows reporting by the various demographic groupings.

So, make up a seven-character identification code. It can be all numbers, all letters, or a combination of numbers and letters. Then write that ID code on the identification line.

In some cases, you may want the participant to record the code by darkening appropriate circles, if provided, on the answer sheet for identification. If so, you have to comply with the specific requirements of the answer sheet.

Now, write that same identification code on the second answer sheet where required.

Check again for questions.

When you have completed your survey, drop the answer sheets in the box by the door as you leave. The booklet and pencils should be placed on the table by the door.

The completed answer sheets will all be sent to (name of tabulator) who will tabulate and report the results. Your completed answer sheets will not be seen by anyone at the company, and after results have been tabulated, they will be destroyed.

Now, a couple of rules: the survey is meant to be completed by individual employees, so no talking with each other. If you must leave the room for any reason before completing the survey, leave all survey materials at your chair. You can take as long as necessary to complete the survey. There is no time limit. The average is about one hour, but some people take more time and some less. If only a part of your survey is completed, only that part will be tabulated.

Check one more time for questions, and then have them begin the survey.

Notification

Once all arrangements have been completed, it is time to notify employees of the survey.

Hopefully, they have been made aware of the company's plans to either initiate a survey or continue its practice of regularly scheduled surveys. However it is accomplished (e-mail, voice mail, memo, bulletin board notice, or newsletter), the important points to communicate are:

The purpose of the survey

The survey format

The date and location of the survey

The importance of full participation

A reference to previous surveys, if appropriate

How and when feedback will occur

Provisions for making up the survey if missed or the survey lost

A procedure to obtain answers to any questions

First Communication

Typically a communication is made to all employees at least one month in advance. It describes the upcoming survey and its purpose. Typical is a notice in an employee newsletter, on a bulletin board, or by e-mail. Ideally, the communication is followed by the signature of the senior executive of the company or is at the company's specific location. For example:

To All Employees

We will be conducting our annual employee opinion survey next month on the fifteenth and the seventeenth. There will be a make-up session on the twenty-second for those unavailable on the scheduled days. Please plan your schedules so you are available one of those three days.

For those who cannot participate any of those days, contact our human resources department to arrange an alternative time.

As in previous years, our survey will be conducted in groups by a representative of an external consulting firm. The results will be tabulated by that firm and a report delivered to all employees within two months of completing the survey.

We have always discovered these surveys to be of assistance in managing the company in a manner that contributes to the best possible working conditions. Your opinions matter, and we look forward to receiving them and working with you to make our company the best it can be.

Your supervisor will be scheduling times for participation.

In the meantime, if you have any questions, contact your supervisor or a human resources person.

To be effective, this type of communication should be preceded by communications to all supervisors. They should be made aware of:

> The survey objective
>
> The format
>
> The dates
>
> Make-up dates
>
> The general administrative procedures
>
> The employee participation schedule
>
> The dates of feedback

If not notified in advance, supervisors are unable to deal with any questions from their employees. That can result in a loss of supervisor support of the survey.

Final Communication

A week or two prior to the survey date, final notification should occur. If you conduct employee opinion surveys on a regular basis, such notification is relatively simple and straightforward. You need only to communicate to employees when, where, and how the survey will be conducted and reported. Also, any changes need to be described. The communication method selected depends on your normal communication system.

If this is the first survey your company has conducted, you need to add some additional words to the first notification.

For written and online surveys, either group or individually administered, that communication could be similar to:

To: _____

On (dates), we will be conducting our employee opinion survey. It will be conducted and the results tabulated by an outside consulting firm. When and where you are to participate will be communicated to you by your supervisor.

If you are unable to participate at your scheduled time, your supervisor can arrange for a make-up time.

We value the opinions of all our employees and hope you will see this as an opportunity to share your thoughts.

As I indicated in my previous communication to you, the results of the survey will be reported to all employees and used as a basis for improving conditions of employment at our company.

If you have any questions, ask your supervisor or a human resources person.

Again, the communication should be over the signature of the senior executive of the company or at the specific location, and it should be preceded by communications to all supervisors.

For mailed surveys, the communication could be similar to:

To: _____

On (dates), you will be mailed our employee opinion survey. You will have complete instructions on how to complete the survey as well as the name of someone to call for assistance.

If you are away during this period or for some other reason cannot participate in that time frame, let your supervisor know as soon as possible. Your supervisor can arrange for a make-up time.

Once completed, you are to return the survey in the accompanying envelope to an outside consulting firm that will tabulate the surveys and report the results.

We value the opinions of all our employees and hope you will see this as an opportunity to share your thoughts.

As I indicated in my previous communication to you, the results of the survey will be reported to all employees and used as a basis for improving conditions of employment at our company.

If you have any questions, ask your supervisor or a human resources person. If you do not receive a survey by _____, call human resources for a replacement.

If the survey is an online one available on any computer, the communication could be similar to:

To: _____

On (dates) our employee opinion survey will be available to you online. However, to access the survey you need a password. This can be obtained from (name). Passwords are randomly assigned and do not identify an individual.

If you are away during this period or for some other reason cannot participate in that time frame, let your supervisor know as soon as possible. Your supervisor can arrange for a make-up time.

Once completed, your responses go to an outside consulting firm that will tabulate the surveys and report the results.

We value the opinions of all our employees and hope you will see this as an opportunity to share your thoughts.

As I indicated in my previous communication to you, the results of the survey will be reported to all employees and used as a basis for improving conditions of employment at our company.

Mailed Written Survey Letter

Although the instructions for a mailed written survey are a part of the survey instrument, there needs to be a general instruction letter accompanying the survey. The following can be used as a guide for creating one:

To: _____

Enclosed you will find our employee opinion survey and answer sheet for your completion. All employees have been mailed similar surveys.

The purpose of the survey to further our ongoing two-way communication and identify areas in which we can work together to make our company an even more ideal working location.

The survey booklet contains the questions. Your responses are to be recorded on the accompanying answer sheet. Use a number two pencil for that purpose. Do not use a pen or colored pencil.

Instructions for completion of the survey and use of the answer sheet appear at the front of the survey booklet. Take a few moments, read the instructions, and respond to the sample questions. If you are unsure of how to record your answers or have any questions, please call _____ before attempting to complete the survey.

The first part of the survey will ask you for some personal information such as department and length of service. These questions are optional. You do not have to answer them, but it is of assistance if you do. They are not questions that can be used to identify you. They are questions whose answers allow group responses to be reported.

For example, assume that employees in one work area were dissatisfied with the lighting. Let's further assume they were ten employees, but in total one hundred employees completed the survey.

If ninety employees were satisfied with their work area lighting, and only these ten were dissatisfied, the dissatisfactions would not be apparent. However, if results are reported by department, the lighting problem will become apparent.

Actually, the personal information cannot be used to identify any one employee. The survey answer sheet does offer a place for your name, but that too is optional. Some employees want to identify themselves. If you are one of those, you may sign, but that is optional. Your name is not required.

There are _____ questions on the survey. You should try to answer them all at one time, so arrange for approximately one hour in a private location. When you have completed the survey, place both the answer sheet and survey booklet in the enclosed addressed and stamped envelope and mail it.

The envelope will be received by an outside consulting firm that will tabulate the survey and report the results. After tabulation, your answer sheet will be destroyed.

For your responses to be included in the survey report, they must be postmarked no later than _____.

If for any reason the booklet or answer sheet is damaged, you may obtain a replacement by calling _____. Just be sure to return the damaged one.

The survey asks for your opinions. There are no correct or incorrect answers—whatever you think is how you should answer. Since it is the answers of each employee that are important, please do not discuss possible responses with others.

Make-Ups

In your preparation, you allowed time for make-up surveys, but there are also some administrative actions to consider.

Some companies contact any employee it knows did not participate in a survey. Some form of communication (memo, voice mail, telephone call, or e-mail) is sent at the conclusion of the survey period. It tells the employee of the make-up procedure and restates the importance of having input from all employees.

If you used employee meetings for completing the survey, you need to advise employees of when and where make-up meetings are to occur. This means you first need to ensure that the facility is reserved, the administrators are scheduled, and supplies are available.

Generally, employees missing focus groups are not rescheduled. However, if a considerable number misses and one or more groups are cancelled, you might consider rescheduling.

Surveys mailed to employees and conducted online can be rescheduled in one of two ways. If you know who has not completed a survey, you can contact them directly. If you do not know, then a general communication to all employees is required. In either case a final date for submission should be stated. Mailed surveys postmarked after that date are not accepted, and the survey is not accessible via computer after that date.

Sometimes an event may cause most employees at one location to miss a scheduled completion meeting. For example, a severe snowstorm or an emergency may result in employees staying home or being required to deal with the emergency. In such an instance, you need to reschedule the survey as soon as possible, and notify all employees of the new date and location.

A Caution

When all surveys are received, they then are given to the tabulator either by you or sent directly by the employees. However, if you are sending them in mass to the tabulator, there is one caution.

A Maryland bank collected at its main human resources office all completed employee opinion surveys from its twelve locations. It then mailed them to a tabulating firm in Minnesota. Unfortunately, they were lost in the mail.

If you must transfer completed surveys, do so by a means that ensures their arrival. The firm in the above bank story had to conduct the survey a second time. The human resources vice president later remarked, "It would have been cheaper to have them hand carried by someone on an airplane."

Conclusion

The final step in administering the survey is to implement it according to your plan. The surveys, as completed, will be received by the tabulator. Your next step is to analyze the reported results from the tabulation.

CHAPTER 11

TABULATING AND COMPILING SURVEY RESULTS

If we do not find anything pleasant, at least we shall find something new.

VOLTAIRE,
Candide

Once survey responses have been tabulated, you will receive a report in the format you requested. Most often, that will consist of:

Populations of employees by total participants and demographics

Question responses by dimensions and subareas

A report broken down by requested demographics

Written responses broken down by departments

Any requested correlations

Any requested comparisons

Any requested comments or analysis

Your first action should be to review the reported results and identify any additional information needed for understanding and analysis.

Response Formats

The format used to report responses to dimensions and questions depends on what the tabulator can provide and what you want. This is something you should decide in advance.

Generally, responses are reported by percentages of those responding to a question. However, they can also be reported as whole numbers. Typically, they are reported in tables or as bar graphs.

Figure 11-1 shows a bar graph reporting responses to an objective (yes/no) question. Reporting is by total employees, department, gender, and length of service.

Figure 11-2 displays bar graphs for responses to dimensions (called factors by the company), and Figure 11-3 displays bar graphs for three questions. Both bar graphs report by percentages of total employees and by three locations.

Past Survey Results

Surveys are best interpreted when compared against some base, and the most useful base is results from a previous employee opinion survey conducted at the same company. However, even that base can be affected by changes.

The base survey should be conducted at the same time of year, with the same number and types of people, measuring the same areas of conditions of employment, and using the same questions and response scales. Changing any of these variables can make the new results less comparable, and if many of the variables are changed, it makes the results almost incomparable.

Earlier in the book, the concept of management by exception was described. Comparison with previous results is an ideal use of this technique. You first look for consistency in results for the same dimensions and demographics. Then if the new results are similar to the previous

(text continues on page 182)

Figure 11-1. Are you notified of job openings in other departments?

Yes/No answers are shown as percentages of those groups responding to the question.

Group	Population	Yes	No	Yes/No
Total	51			86/14
Department A	13			54/46
Department B	28			96/4
Department C	9			100/0
Female	12			58/42
Male	24			96/4
Unidentified Gender	15			93/7
Less than 1 year service	7			85/15
1 year to 5 years	6			83/17
5 years to 10 years	7			71/29
10 years to 15 years	5			100/0
Over 15 years	26			88/12

Figure 11-2. Responses to dimensions.

Percent of Respondents

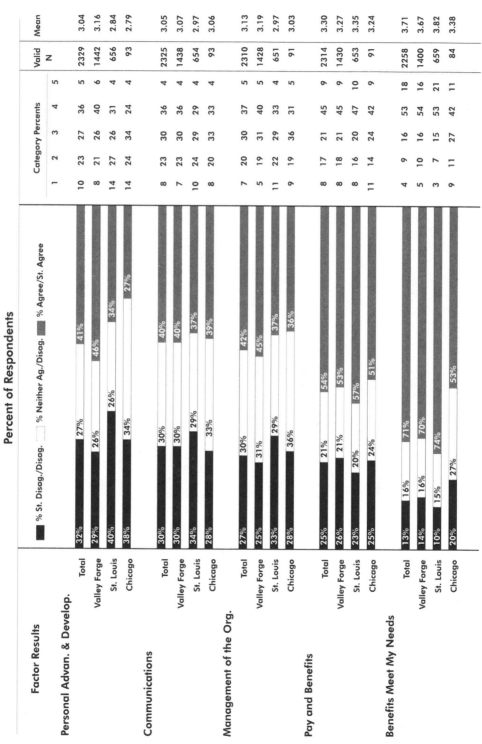

Legend: ■ % St. Disag./Disag. ☐ % Neither Ag./Disag. ■ % Agree/St. Agree

Factor Results		Category Percents					Valid N	Mean
		1	2	3	4	5		
Personal Advan. & Develop.								
	Total	10	23	27	36	5	2329	3.04
	Valley Forge	8	21	26	40	6	1442	3.16
	St. Louis	14	27	26	31	4	656	2.84
	Chicago	14	24	34	24	4	93	2.79
Communications								
	Total	8	23	30	36	4	2325	3.05
	Valley Forge	7	23	30	36	4	1438	3.07
	St. Louis	10	24	29	29	4	654	2.97
	Chicago	8	20	33	33	4	93	3.06
Management of the Org.								
	Total	7	20	30	37	5	2310	3.13
	Valley Forge	5	19	31	40	5	1428	3.19
	St. Louis	11	22	29	33	4	651	2.97
	Chicago	9	19	36	31	5	91	3.03
Pay and Benefits								
	Total	8	17	21	45	9	2314	3.30
	Valley Forge	8	18	21	45	9	1430	3.27
	St. Louis	8	16	20	47	10	653	3.35
	Chicago	11	14	24	42	9	91	3.24
Benefits Meet My Needs								
	Total	4	9	16	53	18	2258	3.71
	Valley Forge	5	10	16	54	16	1400	3.67
	St. Louis	3	7	15	53	21	659	3.82
	Chicago	9	11	27	42	11	84	3.38

Figure 11-3. Bar graphs for three questions.

Percent of Respondents

Legend: ■ % St. Disag./Disag. □ % Neither Ag./Disag. ▨ % Agree/St. Agree

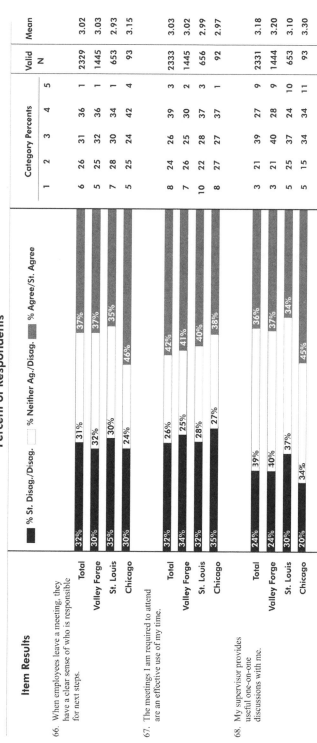

Item Results		Category Percents					Valid N	Mean
		1	2	3	4	5		
66. When employees leave a meeting, they have a clear sense of who is responsible for next steps.	Total	6	26	31	36	1	2329	3.02
	Valley Forge	5	25	32	36	1	1445	3.03
	St. Louis	7	28	30	34	1	653	2.93
	Chicago	5	25	24	42	4	93	3.15
67. The meetings I am required to attend are an effective use of my time.	Total	8	24	26	39	3	2333	3.03
	Valley Forge	7	26	25	30	2	1445	3.02
	St. Louis	10	22	28	37	3	656	2.99
	Chicago	8	27	27	37	1	92	2.97
68. My supervisor provides useful one-on-one discussions with me.	Total	3	21	39	27	9	2331	3.18
	Valley Forge	3	21	40	28	9	1444	3.20
	St. Louis	5	25	37	24	10	653	3.10
	Chicago	5	15	34	34	11	93	3.30

ones and there is a consistent pattern, you can fairly assume the new results represent little change in employee opinion.

However, if the new results are significantly different, you can assume something has occurred to affect opinions. This may be a situation requiring additional information to fully understand and to discover the reasons for the apparent change in opinion.

On the other hand, if prior results varied greatly from year to year, and the new results also vary, it will be difficult to make meaningful comparisons. However, you still may wish to consider focus groups and/or interviews to attempt to discover the reasons for the continual variations. They may provide information to help you adjust the survey for future years and eliminate the inconsistencies.

Other Comparisons

If your company has no previous surveys with which to compare, you can compare your survey results with those from similar industries, size companies, competitors, or companies in the same geographic area. If you do this, attempt to compare with companies that are the most similar to your company and only use dimensions that are defined as your dimensions are. Also, be aware of any conditions that may be affecting the comparison companies, such as reductions in force, expansion of operations, and legal problems.

Response Intensity

Another condition to consider is the degree of response intensity. If you use a five-point scale (or other odd-numbered scale as recommended) and report responses as three basic categories: negative, positive, and neither positive or negative, an even distribution would put one-third of the responses in each category. However, in most cases, you will receive most responses in one of or both the positive and negative categories.

A great deal of neutral responses may indicate the participants do not understand the question or don't care. Equal negative and positive responses or a very high percentage of negative responses also indicates further information is required. In all cases, this may identify areas to explore through focus groups and/or interviews.

Importance and Satisfaction

If you use importance and satisfaction questions for the dimensions, comparing them by dimension can provide insight into which areas should be first considered for additional information. Here, you want to place them in four categories:

High importance and high satisfaction

High importance and low satisfaction

Low importance and low satisfaction

Low importance and high satisfaction

Your want to concentrate on dimensions that receive high importance and low satisfaction ratings and any areas that moved into that category. The areas of low importance and low satisfaction are areas you can generally postpone, and the high satisfaction areas probably require little immediate attention.

Correlations

Finally, there are internal correlations you may have requested. Even without correlations being calculated, you can look for consistency among responses to different types of questions for the same dimension and subarea and the relationship between dimension overall ratings and ratings for the company. The latter can provide a further indication of the importance of conditions of employment to employees.

Additional Information

Using the above as guidelines, you want to review the initial survey tabulation to identify what additional information is required. The areas to review are:

Changes from prior surveys

Responses that conflict or are inconsistent

Differences with any external results

Written comments that refer to unidentified factors

Tabulators' comments

Areas receiving exceptionally negative responses

Changes from Prior Surveys

If your tabulating firm has that information and includes the comparisons in your report, you can quickly note any differences from previous surveys—any exceptions. If the tabulating firm did not have such information but it is available within your company, you will have to make the comparisons. You do so by comparing responses to similar questions in the surveys. Where you discover differences, you need to determine if these are understandable or additional information is required.

Below are the positive results to a question on training from annual surveys conducted over the past five years.

Year 1	Year 2	Year 3	Year 4	This Year
62%	59%	61%	60%	44%

Unless you know of something that has occurred within the company that might impact perception of training or there is additional information in the survey results, this is an area that appears to require more information in order to understand it.

Responses That Conflict or Are Inconsistent

If you requested the tabulator to calculate correlations between elements of the survey, these should be reviewed for low correlations. If there is a high degree of correlation between employee responses to most dimensions but a very low correlation in responses to two dimensions, review the individual questions for those dimensions. Perhaps those responses will identify why there is such a difference or the need for more information.

Even if correlations were not calculated, you can review the responses for inconsistencies. For example, if all benefits are perceived positively except one or two, you may want to investigate why those are perceived less positively.

Differences with Any External Results

Comparing survey results with results from other companies is not as valuable as comparing them with past surveys from your company. However, external comparisons can sometimes indicate areas to investigate. For example, if you have information from surveys conducted at several companies in your geographic area, and they all indicate an increase in positive responses for questions on job security but your employees' responses were very negative, this is an area to consider for further investigation.

Written Comments That Refer to Unidentified Factors

Another source to review is the employees' written comments, if they were requested. Sometimes, such comments are quite specific, but other times, they refer to factors that are not readily identifiable. These you should also note for further consideration.

Tabulators' Comments

If you requested tabulators' comments or analysis, or if the survey was conducted for you by a consultant or consulting firm, your initial report may include the identification of items requiring additional information. Even if you did not request comments or analysis, if something stands out to the tabulator, it may receive a comment.

Areas Receiving Exceptionally Negative Responses

You also should review those areas of the survey that received very negative responses or a high percentage of neutral responses. These may be interpretable, or they may require additional information.

Sometimes, questions receiving high neutral responses are poorly worded. The employees did not understand the question, so they took the neutral position.

Analyzing

Once you have a list of areas that may require additional information, you should do a bit of checking. There are conditions that may explain what occurred and eliminate the need to pursue further information:

> Are there any internal or external actions or factors?
>
> Do written responses provide information for other areas?

If, after considering the above two questions, you still feel additional information is required to understand the survey results, you can use interviews or focus groups. Actually, some companies hold focus groups or interviews even when they have no specific additional information needs identified. They do so to obtain more of the reasoning behind survey results.

Figure 11-4 features an Additional Information Identification form. You can use one of these forms to describe each item of additional information you require and your plan for obtaining it.

The first heading on the form is Information Needed. Here, you should describe what you need to know.

Using the earlier example of a change in the positive perceptions of training, the description might be:

> Why the employees' positive perceptions of training declined this year from past surveys.

From Whom to Obtain Additional Information

The next item on the form is headed Source. Here, you are to describe from whom you can probably seek such information.

An examination of the demographic reports will indicate whether the information is required for just one or two demographic groups or for all employees. For example, you may discover that you only require additional information from the third shift employees at one location to understand their responses to job assignment questions. Or you may require additional information from all employees to understand their responses to advancement opportunity questions.

Figure 11-4. Additional information identification.

Information Needed

Source

Procedure

Number

Which Procedure to Use

The next heading on the form is Procedure. Here, you indicate the procedure or method you plan to employ to obtain the information. Basically, the same formats as used for surveys are available to you. However, to obtain additional information to understand the initial responses received, the interview and focus groups are generally the most effective approaches. Both of these allow for more follow-up and in-depth questioning.

Both approaches require someone skilled in these techniques, and in a survey follow-up session you should always use an external person. If not conducted properly, these can be perceived as interrogation sessions designed to challenge employee survey perceptions.

The considerations for which method to use are the same as described for these two methods as survey approaches. Interviews can provide in-depth information and allow for a great number of follow-up questions. However, they generally require an hour to conduct, and an interviewer can only meet with one person at a time.

Focus groups also provide in-depth information, but follow-up questions within the group process are not as effective as an interview. However, focus groups allow for more participation, and a single leader can meet with up to twelve employees at one time. So, which should you use?

Base your decision on:

> The qualifications available—interviewing skills and/or focus group leadership skills
>
> The size of the population from whom you seek information
>
> The degree of in-depth information you require

Selecting Specific Employees for Follow-Ups

Selection of employees for follow-ups can generally not be done until after the initial survey results are received. Then you can identify the additional information required and, sometimes, from whom to seek it. An exception is when a decision is made to conduct follow-ups with employees drawn from the entire population to obtain general information rather than specifically identified information needs.

For example, if the survey indicated that all employees at one location were dissatisfied with a single condition of employment but all other employees were satisfied, at the very least a follow-up should be conducted with the employees who were dissatisfied.

A manufacturing company with three locations conducted an annual employee opinion survey with all employees. One of the areas surveyed was job security. Two of the locations responded with similar opinions as in past surveys, but one location indicated a significant drop in employee satisfaction with their job security.

The company's management could not identify any reason for such a change, so they decided to use a random sample of employees from that location in focus groups.

They did and discovered the reason—an untrue rumor that the company was going to move the plant. Management quickly responded by assuring employees no relocation was being considered.

You also need to recognize the possible ramifications of who is included and how the objective for the procedure is communicated.

A small Arizona mutual funds company conducted an employee opinion survey. The results indicated the employees between fifty-six and sixty-five years old perceived working conditions far more negatively than all other employees. Since there were only ten employees in that age group, the company decided to have a focus group conducted with all ten.

The focus group was led by a representative of the company's consulting firm. The results indicated these employees were reacting to a change in the starting times. They all felt the time had been unnecessarily changed without allowing any input from employees. The new time prohibited their involvement in a late afternoon seniors program at the local YMCA.

However, by including only employees over fifty-five years old in the group, the employees felt they were being singled out and having their perceptions challenged. Soon a rumor traveled throughout the company that the employee opinion survey was really conducted to get rid of older employees.

As a general rule, survey follow-ups are better conducted with portions of an employee population rather than the entire group. Random sampling can be used to determine which ones to include.

You want to select from the appropriate population, but you also want to ensure each employee in the population has an equal chance of being selected. Otherwise, the results can be skewed.

On the form after the heading Number, indicate how many employees from the source you identified will be either interviewed or asked to participate in a focus group. You are now ready for whatever procedure you selected: the interview or the focus group. The following are the types of preparations and procedures these two approaches utilize.

The Interview

Key to a successful survey follow-up interview is a clear description of what additional information is required and identification of which areas to question. The interviewer also needs to know the basis for requesting the additional information.

Questions

Questions are the main tool of the interviewer, and they should be carefully planned to obtain the information required. You do not want the interview to begin with a question such as:

> Why are you dissatisfied with our compensation program?

That type of approach will probably be perceived as threatening. You are demanding justification of the employee's opinion. Instead you want the questions to be answered openly and honestly, and that is best accomplished when the interviewee does not feel threatened or challenged.

Questions should be not answerable in one word. If they are, it puts the interviewer in the position of pushing for an explanation. So instead of asking:

> Do you feel our health insurance is adequate?

You might ask:

> What type of health insurance do you feel an employee requires?

Questions should not communicate a desired answer. For example, instead of asking:

> We think our company offers an excellent retirement program; what do you think about it?

Ask:

> What are the best and poorest elements of our company's retirement program?

Questions should be prepared to obtain the information you require. Below is a series of questions prepared for a follow-up interview whose objective was to discover the basis for negative responses to questions about career opportunities at the company.

> Our recent employee opinion survey indicated a less-than-positive perception regarding career opportunities at our company. Based on your experience here, how do you feel about the available opportunities?
>
> How do you perceive the opportunities here as meeting your career objectives?
>
> What can be done to improve career opportunities?
>
> What do you feel concerns most employees about the availability of career opportunities?

Survey follow-up interviews are conducted to gather information, so the interviewer needs to project a neutral, interested, and open manner. The interviewer should not argue, indicate disagreement or agreement with answers, or defend the company. All information given should be accepted.

Focus Groups

When you have a number of people from whom to obtain information on the same subject, a focus group meeting is an efficient and effective approach. As with interview preparation, a clear understanding of the information sought is important. The major difference from the interview is determining who should attend any one focus group.

Focus groups are most productive when the participants are at the same level within the organization and have approximately the same degree of knowledge. When determining which of the randomly selected employees are to attend a meeting, these factors must be considered. However, do not attempt to have the meeting membership represent specific opinions. Include a random sample of people.

A typical focus group's procedure is:

> State the objective
>
> Be sure everybody knows everybody
>
> Begin with a nonthreatening information-gathering exercise.
>
> Encourage equal participation
>
> End with a summary of the information and a statement of what you will do next

Following these steps, a focus group conducted to obtain information of annual performance reviews might follow a guide similar to this:

First, thank you for your recent participation in our employee opinion survey. Based on the results of that survey, several meetings are being held with employees to obtain information to better understand some of the responses.

The employees attending these meetings have been randomly selected. Your selection has nothing to do with your survey responses.

The objective for our meeting is to identify the strengths and areas of needed improvement of the annual performance review program.

Let's begin with each of you writing on a piece of paper what you believe are the three best features of the annual performance review program and the three features that most need improvement.

Give them time to write this.

Now, with what you have written, indicate how satisfied you feel most employees are with the program meeting their needs. Use a 1 to 9 scale for that purpose. 1 is very dissatisfied; 5 is neither satisfied nor dissatisfied; 9 is very satisfied. You may use any point on the scale. Please do not use fractions or decimals.

Give them a moment to write their responses.

Finally, write at the bottom of the page how important you feel the program is to most employees. Again, we will use a nine-point scale. 1 is unimportant, 5 is neither important nor unimportant, and 9 is very important.

Give them a moment to write their responses.

Now, fold your paper in half and give it to me.

Shuffle the responses and randomly redistribute them. Then divide the participants into groups of three.

*I want you to meet in your groups and, based on the slips of paper
just distributed to you and your own perceptions, arrive at a group
decision as to the three best features, three features most requiring
improvements, a satisfaction number, and an importance number
for our annual performance review program.*

Allow fifteen to twenty minutes for this activity. Then reconvene the
entire group.

*Okay, let's see where we are. Each group report on your decisions,
beginning with the three best features and the three areas requiring
improvement.*

As the groups give their reports, write the features on a chart pad or
chalkboard using key words, and write the areas requiring improvement
in a similar fashion but in a separate list. If there are differences, allow
discussion by using questions such as:

What are the differences?

What are the similarities?

Next, have each group read the satisfaction number. Write these in a
column. Then have each group read the importance number in the same
order so the importance numbers can be written in a second column next
to the satisfaction numbers.

Depending on the answers you receive, ask questions such as:

What are the major points of satisfaction? Of dissatisfaction?

What changes do you feel are most required?

What are the employee needs that the program is not fulfilling?

If there has been a change in preceptions since previous surveys, you
can ask:

How has the program changed during the past year?

Are there any changes at our company that have affected the program?

You need to remain flexible. You are conducting the meeting to obtain information. Sometimes, the information may lead to subjects other than the objective. You want to allow free discussion if it relates at all to the survey and its results.

Conclude by thanking the participants and telling them the information they provided will be used in the survey report.

Conclusion

You now have the initial tabulator's report. You have identified additional information required to understand the report, and you have obtained that information. Chapter 12 will examine considerations for using external services and products.

CONSIDERING EXTERNAL SERVICES AND PRODUCTS

When all else fails, read the instructions.

AGNES ALLEN,
Omni

Thus far, this book has reviewed the steps required to develop and conduct a successful employee opinion survey. It is something that can be accomplished solely by company personnel, solely by an external service, or by a mix of the two. To decide what the best approach is for your company, you need to consider a number of factors: internal personnel, credibility, timeliness, valid instrument, and comparison data.

Internal Personnel

To develop a survey instrument, administer it, and tabulate results requires both available time and the necessary abilities. If

197

these are not available within your company, you should not consider tackling such a project. However, you may have the internal expertise and time to implement certain aspects of the survey such as the identification of dimensions. In such a situation, you could contract for the portions you are unable to do.

Credibility

As mentioned a number of times in this book, the greatest advantage in using an external service is credibility. It projects objectivity into survey tabulation and maintains the confidentiality of responses.

> A New Jersey pharmaceutical company decided to use its own data-processing group to tabulate its employee opinion survey. In developing the survey and its administration procedures, the human resources department had stressed the need for confidentiality.
>
> However, one of the data processors discussed some of the survey responses with his friends. The confidentiality of individual employee responses was not breached, but other employees soon knew a data processor was talking about the survey. All confidence in confidentiality was lost.

Timeliness

If you tackle some of the implementation of the survey, you have to consider timeliness. You not only have to factor in the time it takes internal personnel to work on the project, but you also have to consider whether they can meet the required completion date. Employees unfamiliar with the process may take considerably more time to complete it than an experienced person would. Most employees have other responsibilities and may not be able to devote enough hours to the project.

Valid Instrument

Even when an external firm customizes a survey instrument for a company, it generally uses an existing instrument as a base. Such instruments have probably been tested over a period of time. Their questions have been regularly reviewed and revised, and validity and reliability studies have been conducted. The result is a survey instrument that is error-free and effective.

Comparison Data

The most useful data with which to compare survey results are data from your company's past surveys. If an external firm has that data and you do not, staying with that firm has an advantage. If this is your first survey, there is no prior data for your company. You may want to compare results with those from other companies. A firm that regularly conducts surveys probably can provide such data.

Should You Use an External Service?

Considering the above factors, should you use an external service or do it yourself?

Here are our suggestions:

> Use an external service to tabulate and report results even if the survey is conducted online.

> Either have an external firm administer the survey or have completed surveys mailed directly to it.

> Have an external firm conduct any survey focus groups and interviews.

> Considering the earlier factors, decide what remaining portions of the project you want to do and what portions you want an external service to do.

Your Responsibility

Whatever you decide, you should always be in control of all the aspects of the survey. Even if an external firm is contracted to do the entire project, you should approve the dimensions and instrument and describe the report format.

This book has continually stressed the need to clearly identify your objective and your planned use of the survey information. That is your responsibility. An external firm can assist you, but the objective has to be yours. You should not adjust your needs to meet those of an external firm. It is the external firm that is accountable for meeting the needs of your company.

Likewise, the dimensions to be measured need to be the ones associated with your company. If the external firm has a list of dimensions with definitions, consider them, and use them if they apply. However, do not use them in lieu of the dimensions required by your company.

Even if the external firm has a survey instrument that it has used at numerous companies, do not accept it unless it uses questions that relate to your company and covers all aspects of each desired dimension.

Finally, the construction of the survey report should be described by you to meet your company's requirements. Actually, most firms include a process for customizing their survey approach to your company's needs. The important point is that you identify exactly what you want a consultant to do for you.

Publishers

Rather than contracting with an external service, it is possible to purchase employee opinion survey instruments. Some are sold with computer-tabulation and reporting programs. Others must be returned to the supplier for tabulation and reporting. Some are sold solely as survey instruments, and you have to develop your own tabulation and scoring.

A number of industry associations have surveys available for their members' use. These are generally customized for their type of business, but even so, they have to be reviewed to ensure they meet your company's requirements. Often, they can be used "as is" with the addition of a separate set of questions applicable to your company.

Tabulators

There are a number of companies that offer computer tabulation services for employee opinion surveys. Generally, they do no report writing or analysis. They merely receive the completed answer sheets, tabulate them, and report results.

You usually have some options as to the structure of the report. You can request tables, graphs, percentages, or whole numbers.

In most cases, you are required to use one of their form answer sheets. That can be a benefit, but you need to ensure the answer sheet has the proper number of response options and questions.

Although we believe it is better not have your company tabulate survey results, there are also a number of programs available that can tabulate your results, and there are others that can calculate correlations. If you are considering purchasing any of these, you should involve a professional from your data-processing area.

Locating External Assistance

Most large consulting firms either provide employee opinion surveys or can recommend a firm or individual who does. Many independent consultants also provide surveys, but they can be more difficult to locate. Some industrial psychologists also perform such services.

The following are sources for such services (listed in no particular order):

❏ *Industry Associations*. Many of these associations can provide information on firms that have conducted surveys for other companies in your industry. Some associations even recommend firms or offer the service.

❏ *Professional Associations*. Organizations such as the American Management Association, New York, New York, and the Society for Human Resource Management, Alexandria, Virginia, generally will not recommend services but usually can supply a list of people and firms in your area.

❏ *The Yellow Pages*. Look under the headings of consultants, management consultants, and psychologists (industrial or organizational). You may find that some list their areas of specialization.

❏ *The Internet.* Use key words such as employee opinion surveys, consultant, industrial psychologist, and organizational psychologist. More and more individuals and firms are establishing Web sites. You may discover exactly the expertise you require.

❏ *Libraries and Bookstores.* There are several directories of consultants. Probably the best known is the *Directory of Management Consultants*, published by Kennedy Publications and Consultants News, Fitzwilliam, New Hampshire. Another directory is *Consultants and Consulting Organizations,* published by Gale Group, Detroit, Michigan. Both of these provide information on the types of services offered by consultants.

❏ *Universities and Business Schools.* Talk to one of the professors specializing in organizational development, human resources, or a similar topic. She may be able to provide names of professionals in your area.

❏ *Other Companies.* If you know of a company that has conducted a survey, give them a call. They may be able to give you names of what consultants they used and others they considered.

❏ *One of Your Professional Services.* If your company uses professional services such as labor lawyers, benefit consultants, search firms, and accountants, they may be able to supply names. Sometimes, they have people on staff who perform such work. Other times, they may have come in contact with such firms through other clients.

How to Select a Firm

Assuming you have obtained names of individuals and firms, how do you determine which one(s) to use? Here are some considerations, whether you are considering a firm to design and conduct the survey or just to tabulate and report results:

❏ *Check references.* Talk to former clients. Ask how satisfied they were with the services. Check such things as cost, staying within quote, validity and reliability of results, on-time delivery, credibility, and thoroughness. If you obtained the name from another company that used the firm, ask it for a reference.

As a general rule, ask for the names of the last three clients for whom similar services were provided. Then call those clients. Explain your project and ask if they would recommend the individual or firm for it.

❏ *Ask to see a typical survey report.* Most firms do not want to share their questions, but they should be willing to provide a typical report. Review it to determine if it is of the type and quality you desire.

❏ *Check flexibility.* Discover if the firm is capable and willing to adjust their survey instrument and report formats to meet the needs of your company.

❏ *Check services offered.* Does the firm offer complete services or only a portion of those you require?

❏ *Check confidentiality of your information.* If the firm has your survey data, is there a control that ensures it is not shared with other companies without your consent? However, note that most firms will include your information in a database for comparisons but do so in a manner that protects your confidentiality.

❏ *Check for comparable statistics.* Does the firm maintain a database of comparable statistics? If they do, discover for what geographic areas, company sizes, and types of industries they have them. Also, ask for the dates of the information and the number of cases.

❏ *Visit the individual's or firm's office.* The office can tell you a great deal about how the work is accomplished. It communicates the degree of organization, equipment, and support personnel. One caution: There are independent practitioners in this area who work out of an office at home. Many of these people are excellent at what they do, so do not discount them for lacking a formal separate office and staff.

❏ *Talk to more than one consultant.* Each meeting with a prospective service provider will be educational. You will learn not only about them but also more about your project through their questions and suggestions. Be prepared for these meetings. Have your questions ready, and have available all of the answers and materials someone will need in order to give you a proposal. When the meeting begins, state your objective and give any necessary background information. Then turn the meeting over to the consultant. Let him ask the questions he needs. You will discover how thorough the person is, how well your need is understood, and the approach the person uses.

After all the person's questions have been answered, you can then ask yours:

> Can you do the work?
>
> What approaches and methods will be used?
>
> How long will it require?
>
> What type of survey instrument do you use?
>
> Can the instrument be customized?
>
> Have any validation or reliability studies been conducted for the instrument?
>
> What types of report formats are available?
>
> Can the report formats be customized?
>
> For whom has similar work been performed?
>
> What will the service cost?

❏ *Require a written proposal.* Ask for a written proposal that describes how the project will be approached, when it will be completed, and at what cost. Describe the degree of detail you expect. Written proposals should allow for easy comparisons. Also, they provide documentation of all aspects of the project.

Read all proposals carefully. Raise questions about any item you feel is not covered, and request any additional information you feel is required.

❏ *Confirm details.* Be sure you understand when the project will be complete, what you will receive at the conclusion of the project, what the total costs will be, and how expenses are billed and documented.

❏ *Check costs.* If you are unsure of the going rate for such work, check with other companies or compare rates among proposals. Determine if expenses require your prior approval—they should over a certain amount. Also, be sure expenses are invoiced as actual and are not "marked up." An exception here is based on your company's payment practices. If you pay within thirty days of invoicing, expenses should be actual. If you take longer, an extra charge is not unreasonable.

❐ *Check credentials*. Be sure what you are told is correct. If an individual claims some type of certification or specialized training related to the work, check it. If an individual tells you she is a licensed psychologist, confirm it. Such information is a matter of public record, and every so often you will discover a claim of credentials that is untrue.

❐ *Check payment times*. It is not unreasonable for an initial payment to be due at the time work is begun, and if the project continues for several months, interim payments are reasonable. However, the final payment should not be required until the project is completed and all materials and information are delivered to you. The final payment should be of significant size to assist in ensuring completion.

❐ *Discover who will actually perform the work*. You may be very impressed with the knowledge and experience of the person you have met, but is he or she the person who will actually conduct and interpret your survey? Ask who will be administering the survey; who will interpret results; and who will report the results to you, to management, and to the employees.

There should be no hesitation in providing this information. If there is, wait until it is provided before making a commitment. Also, be sure you are satisfied with the answers. You may have to request the credentials of the people.

Contracting

Once you have made your selection, get all the details in writing: cost, expenses, invoicing procedures, payment times, delivery times, and work schedule. Be sure the project as presented will meet your objectives. Include a statement of confidentiality regarding the information obtained about your organization and employees. Such a statement can prohibit disclosure of that information to third parties, including through journal articles and presentations to other clients.

Both parties should sign the document to indicate their agreement to its terms and conditions. Since such a document is binding on the organization, it should be reviewed by your internal legal department or external legal counsel prior to signing.

Products

If you are considering purchasing a survey instrument rather than complete survey services, many of the previous suggestions still apply—particularly if you are considering a product offered by a consultant or consulting firm. However, in most instances, you will probably be dealing with a publisher, and you may be limited to reviewing literature. Here are some methods to contact potential sources:

❒ *Read sales and administrative materials.* Most publishers provide descriptive sales literature. Sometimes it is very complete, but other times it makes general claims with little documentation. Obtaining an administrative manual can often solve this. Also, some publishers have validity and reliability studies available on request.

❒ *Talk to a representative.* Depending on the cost of the product and your potential volume of business, a representative may meet with you. Other times it may be possible to meet with a representative at the publisher's offices. If the product is going to be used on an ongoing and extensive basis, ask if the publisher provides internal validation services.

❒ *Visit conventions.* There are several appropriate national conventions and regional meetings in the training and organizational development fields. Often, these include vendor booths. If the timing is right for you, you can meet with several publishers in one day; compare their products, obtain prices and literature, and ask questions.

How to Select

All of the actions described for a services firm can be used in selecting a publisher to provide a survey instrument. In addition:

❒ *Be cautious of interpretation by the publisher.* There are some products that require they be returned to the publisher for scoring and interpretation. Generally, these should be avoided unless they provide a logical reason for the approach. However, this caution does not apply to a publisher that will machine score tests for you.

Conclusion

Whenever you are embarking on an activity that can affect the employment of others, you want to be confident you have taken the appropriate precautions to ensure the information is valid and reliable. Otherwise, you will be making decisions based on faulty information, so you could spend a great deal of time, money, and other resources and not accomplish the objective.

PART FOUR

REPORTING YOUR EMPLOYEE OPINION SURVEY RESULTS

CHAPTER 13

WRITING AND DELIVERING REPORTS

'Tis not knowing much but what is useful that makes a man wise.

THOMAS FULLER,
Gnomologia

Employee opinion survey reports can take a wide variety of formats. They vary by what is reported, how it is reported, and to whom it is reported. Generally, there are at least two reports for each survey:

A report to management of the initial results

A report to employees of the results and management's reactions

Both reports are based on the tabulated results, the additional information obtained, and any comparisons available. At this point, you have the first two items of information. The third comparison has been mentioned several times—comparisons with previous surveys.

Comparisons

As was mentioned earlier in this book, the results of a survey are not in themselves right or wrong. They are employee opinions, so they are relative. But relative to what?

The best comparison is with results from previous surveys at your company. Other comparisons can be made with survey results from your consultant, industry groups, area associations, and individual companies.

Your Company's Past Survey Results

Results from previous surveys at your company are the best comparison. You have the same dimensions or questions for comparisons.

Consultants' Results

If you are using a consulting firm that regularly conducts surveys, the firm probably has a database of results from similar surveys. If the same dimensions or questions are used, it provides a comparison.

Industry Groups

Some industry groups collect survey results from member companies. Some even publish surveys that are available to their members. Although they will usually not identify which results are from which company, they will often provide results by unidentified companies and collective results for all companies.

Area Associations

In some geographic areas, associations collect data such as survey results and make it available to other companies. Typically, these associations are development groups, employers' groups, and local universities.

Individual Companies

Finally, there are the associations you have made with other companies. For example, in a major metropolitan area of Massachusetts, there are several service companies of similar size. The human resources managers of these companies have agreed to share their employee opinion data with one another. (Actually, it has proved so beneficial that the companies are now sharing compensation and benefit data.)

No Comparison

Okay, but suppose this is your first survey and you can locate no source of comparison data, what should you do? You should report your survey results as statistics with some analysis. Included in your report should be a plan to use these first survey data as bases for future surveys.

Using Comparisons

In Chapter 3, the concept of management by exception was introduced as it applies to comparisons with previous surveys. You may not know what the ideal percentage of positive responses should be, but you can identify changes in the percentages—the exceptions.

Let's assume that 30 percent of your employees perceive the company's compensation program to be very good, and 30 percent of your employees perceive it as requiring improvement. What does that signify? Is it good or bad? Does the program require improvement, or is it doing fine?

If you have surveyed your employees each year for the past five years and each year included compensation program as one area surveyed, you can compare this year's results with previous year's results for that area.

Below are three possible series of results from a question regarding the company's compensation program. Each indicates the positive responses to the same question over a period of five years:

	Year 1	Year 2	Year 3	Year 4	This Year
Example 1	24%	25%	27%	29%	30%
Example 2	35%	33%	33%	32%	30%
Example 3	43%	42%	44%	41%	30%

In the first example, the 30 percent this year indicates a continuing improvement in employees' perceptions regarding the company's compensation program. Example 2 indicates the program is receiving similar reactions each year, but example 3 indicates a significant decline in positive responses.

If comparisons other than previous surveys are available, you might want to consider them, but remember that comparisons with results from previous surveys is the ideal method for identifying changes in perceptions at your company.

Over the years, we have discovered certain tendencies in employee opinion survey results, but they are only tendencies. For example, we have found communication and compensation generally receive lower positive comments than they may deserve—even when facts prove otherwise.

Perhaps it is because no matter how good communication is, there are usually some rumors. With compensation, employees may not want to be too positive since that may be interpreted as saying that increases are not necessary.

Apples to Apples

In any comparison of results, you have to be sure you are comparing similar results—apples to apples. For example, assume you surveyed "security." You defined security as an employee feeling confident he can remain employed with the company as long as he performs well.

You discover a similar company has recently conducted an employee opinion survey that also measures security, so you decide to compare your employees' responses with the ones they received. That could be a good idea if both of you are defining and questioning the same type of security.

If the other company defined security as the feeling of being safe from outside dangers, you will be comparing two completely different securities, even though they both have the same name. It is the definition that counts.

A Maryland-based company conducted its first employee opinion survey. Since they had no previous survey information, they elected to compare their results with those from a utility company in the same community. However, the utility was considering a reduction in workforce, and the employees knew of it. The first company had a stable work environment. The possible reduction in workforce significantly affected the utility company's results, so a comparison was very misleading.

If your company has no previous surveys with which to compare, you may want to discover if there are other types of survey information available. Check with your consultant if you are using one. Check with local associations, industry associations, and local colleges. If you have a relationship with another company in the area that has conducted a survey, see if you can use some of its data. Just keep in mind the cautions mentioned about ensuring similar definitions and questions.

Once you have your comparison data, you are ready to prepare the initial report for management.

Management's Reactions and Action Plans

Your ultimate aim should be the report for all employees, but to be meaningful, your report should contain management's reactions to the survey information. Otherwise, it can create more questions and concerns than it answers.

A Louisiana-based electrical products manufacturer conducted its first employee opinion survey. All responses were calculated as percentages of those responding. The plant manager called a meeting of all employees and presented the results.

At the conclusion of the presentation, he asked for questions. The first question was, "What does that all mean?"

Unfortunately, the plant manager did not know how to answer the question. The next question was, "It looks like employees are dissatisfied with their pay. What is the company going to do to correct that?"

The Management Report Structure

There is no one correct structure for an initial report to management. Most initial reports include:

> Description of the survey, its objectives, its dimension, number and types of questions, and demographics of those taking the survey
>
> Graphs or tables of each dimension for all employees and for major demographic groupings
>
> Commentary on dimension reports
>
> Graphs or tables of specific questions that differ significantly from past surveys, dimension results from all employees, and/or very negative or neutral responses (Generally, we consider negative or neutral responses above 20 percent as significant for inclusion.)
>
> Commentary on individual questions
>
> Comparisons with previous survey results or comparisons with external surveys, if available
>
> Display of the relationship of dimension satisfaction responses to importance responses
>
> Plan for communicating results to employees

In the report, all of the statistical information and written comments are included.

Another area to consider is the degree of intensity. If you use a five-point scale (or other odd-numbered scale as recommended), you can consider the three basic points of the scale: strong negative, strong positive, and neutral. An even distribution would put one-third of the responses in each category. However, in most cases, you will receive most responses in one of or both the two endpoints.

A great deal of neutral responses may indicate that the participants do not understand the question or don't care. Equal numbers of negative and positive responses also raise questions. In either case, this may be an area to explore through focus groups and/or interviews.

Generally, the report to management is delivered as both a written executive summary with supporting documentation and an oral report to the appropriate group of senior managers. Typically, an oral report includes overhead slides of key points and graphs. This approach allows for questions and discussion.

The objective at a meeting with senior managers is to obtain management's comments and action plans regarding the survey results. For example, assume the survey indicates that employees' satisfaction with the benefit program decreased over the past year. However, management believes the company is competitive. The reaction to the survey item might be:

We are disappointed that our employees believe our benefit program is not competitive with other companies in the area. Our policy is to offer a competitive benefit program, so during the next two months, our human resources department will conduct a survey of benefits offered by local companies. The results of that survey will be communicated to all employees. If those results indicate we are no longer competitive, we can consider what adjustments can be made to ensure we remain competitive within the budget available for benefits.

Other times, it may not be possible to take any action. If that is the case, the best reaction is the truth.

We were disappointed to discover employees are dissatisfied with office hours. The early starting time appears to be the area of greatest dissatisfaction. However, we are not certain much can be done about that.

We are a Western-based company with the majority of our customers based on the East Coast. Our customers are three hours ahead of us, and they tend to contact us at the start of their work-day. That means we have to be available when they call.

It is true that some departments do not deal with customers, but they need to be available at the same time other employees are at work.

Early starting times appear to be a necessary condition of employment, so we do not envision changing them in the future. If you have an individual problem, you should speak with your supervisor or the human resources department.

Often, the initial report is written by the consultant who is conducting the survey. However, an external consultant cannot know all of the internal situations, so comments from someone within the organization are required. In some companies, the person in charge of the survey often includes suggested language in the initial report for wording management's reaction.

At times, a suggestion may be made to change the reported survey results or to not report certain results. To do either of these things is almost always a mistake. If management wants to receive open, truthful communication from employees, it must provide the same type of communication to them. A sample management summary report is explained in Chapter 14.

The Employee Report Structure

With management's reactions known, a final report can be written. This will be a report that is communicated to all employees. It does not have to be as detailed as the report to management, but it should include:

Description of the survey, its objective, its dimension, number and types of questions, and demographics of those taking the survey

Graphs, tables, or comments of each dimension for all employees

Commentary on dimension reports

Comparisons with previous survey results or comparisons with external surveys, if available

Display of the relationship of dimension satisfaction responses to importance responses

Management's reactions and action plans based on the survey results

The report to employees can take many shapes and be delivered in many ways. The two most generally used are meetings and a printed document.

All-Employee Meetings

Where possible, we prefer to deliver the report to employees through meetings. The number required varies by company, but where such meetings are held, they usually consist of:

Presentation of the survey results by the person responsible for its analysis (This is usually accomplished by projecting the graphs or tables onto a screen.)

Management's reactions to the survey results presented by someone from senior management

Depending on the size of the group, questions may be possible, but it is more effective to conduct and schedule follow-up meetings with smaller numbers of employees when necessary.

The Booklet

Some companies publish a small report booklet that is distributed to all employees. Some use a lengthy memo. Some report by e-mail, some in the employee newsletter, and some by video. The medium you select is what is appropriate and generally used for employee communication.

Legal Review

However you elect to report the survey results to employees, be sure to review with your attorney what you will say or write. This will allow you to avoid what could be a costly mistake.

An Alabama manufacturing plant conducted an employee opinion survey. One of the issues addressed was employee dissatisfaction with the compensation program. In a printed pamphlet sent to all employees, the company reported the survey results and included comments from management. One comment was:

We were disappointed to learn employees are not satisfied with the current compensation program. Based on comments provided, it appears that many feel we pay below the going-rate for similar jobs in our area.

Our policy is to pay a wage that is at least equal to wages for similar jobs in our area. Within the next month, we will conduct and publish the results of a compensation survey made with similar companies in our area.

Management conducted the promised compensation survey, but discovered they were paying less than other companies. Not wanting to admit this, they decided not to publish the results.

One employee filed suit, first to have the results published, and later to have the company pay as per its commitment.

Conclusion

The next chapter discusses sample management reports. It is followed by Chapter 15, which shows two samples of reports given to employees. The first is a report that was delivered to all employees in a special edition of the employee newsletter. The second report was prepared as a separate booklet.

CHAPTER 14

SAMPLE MANAGEMENT SUMMARY REPORTS

Our knowledge is a little island in a great ocean of nonknowledge . . .

ISAAC BASHEVIS SINGER,
The New York Times, December 3, 1978

This chapter contains portions of two management reports of the results from employee opinion surveys.

First Report

The first report is for a small New England HMO. It describes the results from the survey that was earlier supplied as a sample (Chapter 9).

The company was only six years old at the time of the survey. The results reflect the conditions and programs of that company at that time. The entire report consisted of 168 pages of statistics, 110 pages of written comments, and an executive summary. Only the executive summary is supplied in this chapter.

There was a separate page of statistics for each question on the survey. Each question was restated, followed by the percentages of employees responding positively, neutrally, and negatively to the question. The same percentages were shown for the demographic groups. All were shown in a table as bar graphs.

Each page of the written comments contained the response to the essay question from one employee. The pages were grouped by department.

The executive summary was the basis for an initial evaluation and discussion of the results by the top management group. Later, reactions to the summary were developed and communicated to all employees.

An Executive Summary of the Annual Employee Opinion Survey

Introduction

On (dates), all of the employees were offered the opportunity to participate in the annual employee opinion survey. The survey consisted of 163 multiple-choice questions and one question requesting a written response. The questions were based on previous employee opinion surveys and recommendations received this past year from employees.

A representative of the employee opinion survey consulting firm administered the survey to groups of approximately _____ employees each. In total, 210 employees completed the survey. The consulting firm also tabulated the survey results.

On (dates), focus group sessions were conducted by a representative from the employee opinion survey consulting firm. The groups consisted of between six and twelve employees each. These groups were designed to obtain additional information based on an initial analysis of the survey results.

196 employees participating in the survey supplied written answers.

All 196 employees participating in the survey supplied an answer to the essay question.

The month following the survey, four focus groups of randomly selected employees were conducted. These were constructed to obtain additional information based on an initial review of the statistical results of the survey.

This report includes the results and analyses by the employee opinion consulting firm of the annual employee opinion survey.

Demographics

The 210 employees who participated in the survey represented 92 percent of the total employees as of the date of the survey. The survey requested some identifying data: length of service, employee classification, and department. The number of employees by each of these categories appears below.

By Employee Group	Number
Executive	7
Management	13
Supervisor	18
Professional	71
Clerical	59
Other	22

By Length of Service	
Six months or less	14
More than six months to one year	35
More than one year to three years	90
More than three years to five years	30
More than five years	23

By Departments

Total Finance	19
Finance	11
Information Services	7
Other Finance	1
Total Health Services	64
Provider Relations/Wellness	19
Health Care Management	27
Medical, Quality, and Risk Management	6
Utilization Review	8
Other Health Services	4
Total Administration	64
Claims/COB	33
Group Administration/Billing	17
Office Services/Claims Control	11
Other Administration	3
Total Marketing	34
Member Services	14
Sales and Service	10
Other Marketing	10
All Other Departments	15

Dimensions

The questions on the survey represented sixteen employment-related dimensions. The sixteen dimensions were:

Overall Company

Company Policies

Job Performance

Fairness and Responsibility

Training and Development

Job Security

Supervision

Change

Communication

Compensation

Benefits

Department Procedures

Opportunity for Advancement

Executive Management

Quality Customer Service

Recognition

There were satisfaction and importance questions for each dimension and for individual benefits.

The questions contained in the annual employee opinion survey were somewhat different from those in previous surveys. The new questions reflected:

A reexamination of the purpose for which employee opinion surveys were conducted.

An identification of additional areas for which information was desired.

Input from the employees.

The Fairness and Responsibility dimension replaced, both in name and content, the former Equal Treatment dimension. The Quality Customer Service and Recognition dimensions were new. Satisfaction questions had been included in prior surveys but were allocated among the dimensions. In this survey, the satisfaction questions were expanded and reported together. The importance questions were new to this survey.

Results

The following list indicates the percentage of positive responses from all employees by dimension.

Dimension	Percentage of Positive Responses
Overall Company	76
Company Policies	53
Job Performance	70
Fairness and Responsibility	52
Training and Development	38
Job Security	69
Supervision	61
Change	41
Communication	35
Compensation	39
Benefits	83
Department Procedures	57
Opportunity for Advancement	36
Executive Management	56
Quality Customer Service	72
Recognition	55

New to this survey were questions asked in the areas of importance and satisfaction. Actually, these two areas included both all other dimensions and benefits alone. Those results are shown below by the percentage of positive responses.

Benefit Satisfaction	61
Benefit Importance	75
All Dimensions Satisfaction	52
All Dimensions Importance	93

Although the questions in the dimensions changed significantly this year, there will probably be some interest in comparing this year's results with previous years' survey results. For that purpose, a table has been prepared, but it is supplied with a caution. Although the specific questions changed within each dimension, there still is a similarity in construction, so comparisons can be made only on the most general basis.

Percentage of Positive Responses by Dimension

	3 Years Ago N=69	2 Years Ago N=102	Last Year N=138	This Year N=196
Overall Company	49%	72%	62%	76%
Company Policies	20%	42%	47%	53%
Job Performance	62%	71%	69%	70%
Department Procedures	53%	59%	52%	57%
Supervision	57%	65%	60%	61%
Job Security	55%	69%	69%	69%
Compensation	*	*	26%	39%
Benefits	*	*	80%	83%
Communication	42%	66%	58%	35%
Executive Management	64%	76%	76%	56%
Fairness and Responsibility	**	**	65%	52%
Opportunity for Advancement	**	**	47%	36%
Change	25%	46%	36%	41%
Training and Development	14%	33%	21%	38%

*In the surveys of two and three years ago, Compensation and Benefits were combined as one dimension, Pay and Benefits.

**In the surveys of two and three years ago, for Fairness and Responsibility and Opportunity for Advancement were combined as one dimension, Equal Treatment/Opportunity to Advance.

Since it was impossible to compare this year's survey results by dimension with previous surveys, key questions from each dimension that remained relatively unchanged were compared. Those comparisons, by dimension, for this year's and the previous two years' surveys follow.

	2 Years Ago	Last Year	This Year
Overall Company			
I am proud to work for our company.	89%	85%	96%
How do you rate our company as a place to work compared with other companies you know about?	86%	80%	84%
All things considered, how satisfied are you with our company?	76%	67%	76%
Company Policies			
All things considered, how do you rate our company's employee policies and procedures?	45%	33%	60%
Company employee policies are administered the same in all departments.	43%	19%	29%
Job Performance			
All things considered, how satisfied are you with your job?	73%	64%	68%
Fairness* and Responsibility			
All things considered, how do rate the fairness with which our company treats all employees?	43%	38%	49%

*It should be noted that in the surveys of two and three years ago, Equal Treatment was used instead of Fairness.

	2 Years Ago	Last Year	This Year
Training and Development			
I am satisfied with the training provided for my current job.	55%	32%	43%
I am satisfied with the amount of training offered for advancement.	24%	17%	43%
All things considered, how do you rate the overall training and development provided?	31%	15%	40%
Job Security			
All things considered, how do rate the job security provided by our company?	76%	73%	69%
Supervision			
My supervisor is competent in human relations.	57%	54%	64%
All things considered, how do you rate the supervision you receive?	59%	57%	54%
Change			
All things considered, how satisfied are you with the amount of change occurring within our company?	68%	56%	45%

The wording of questions in this dimension were changed so greatly, it was difficult to provide further comparisons.

	2 Years Ago	Last Year	This Year
Communication			
How do you rate the amount of communication you receive from our company?	79%	73%	38%
All things considered, how do rate the overall communication at our company?	57%	46%	23%
Compensation			
How do you rate the total cash compensation you receive compared to what you could receive for similar work from another company in the area?*	30%	26%	34%
How do you rate the relationship between the amount of compensation you receive and your performance?	49%	43%	32%
Benefits			
All things considered, how do you rate our company's overall benefits?	80%	80%	80%
Department Procedures			
My department is well organized for the work it does.	58%	43%	60%
Opportunity for Advancement			
I feel there is adequate opportunity for me to move to a better job within our company.	27%	21%	32%
How do you rate your long-term career potential at our company?	53%	54%	46%
Executive Management			
All things considered, how do you rate the quality of our customer service?	71%	66%	38%

*In prior years "salary" was used in place of "total cash compensation" for this question.

Importance/Satisfaction

For each of the dimensions, two questions were asked:

How important is (name of the dimension) to you?

How satisfied are you with (name of the dimension) at our company?

The following list indicates the relationship of the satisfaction and importance questions for each dimension:

High Importance and High Satisfaction

Job Security

Fairness and Responsibility

Company Policies

Benefits

Job Performance

Department Procedures

High Importance and Low Satisfaction

Compensation

Recognition

Training and Development

Change

Low Importance and Low Satisfaction

Opportunity for Advancement

Quality Customer Service

Low Importance and High Satisfaction

Supervision

Overall Company

Also, these same two questions were asked for each of the bene-fits currently offered by the company. The results are:

High Importance and High Satisfaction

Employee Health Care Coverage

Prescription Drug Plan

Short-Term Disability Insurance

Employee Life Insurance

Vision Benefits

Time Away from Work

Employee Dental Insurance

Long-Term Disability Insurance

Flexible Work Hours

Dependant Health Care Coverage

Tuition Reimbursement

High Importance and Low Satisfaction

Pension Plan

Gainsharing

Dependant Dental Insurance

Low Importance and Low Satisfaction

Eyeglasses Discount

Dependant Life Insurance

Employee Referral Plan

Employee Assistance Plan

Additional Employee Life Insurance

Travel Insurance

Low Importance and High Satisfaction

Accidental Death and Dismemberment Insurance

Write-In Benefit Responses

On the written response sheets, participants were asked to indicate how they would allocate ninety dollars toward the purchase of benefits. They were told each benefit costs ten dollars.

The following table indicates the number of ten-dollar responses to a benefit:

Employee Life Insurance	107.0
Additional Employee Life Insurance	14.0
Dependant Life Insurance	25.0
AD&D	22.0
Travel Insurance	3.0
Vision Benefits	92.5
Eyeglasses Discount Insurance	34.0
Time Away from Work	111.0 *
Employee Dental Insurance	166.0
Dependant Dental Insurance	82.0
Day Care Center	47.0 **
Employee Health Insurance	175.5
Dependant Health Insurance	112.5
Pension Plan	152.5 ***
Gainsharing	90.5
Short-Term Disability Insurance	133.5
Long-Term Disability Insurance	97.5
Cash	89.0 ****
Employee Assistance Plan	15.5
Prescription Drug Plan	155.5

* Four people allocated eighteen dollars each to this benefit.

** One person allocated all money to this benefit.

*** Three people allocated eighteen dollars or more each to this benefit.

**** Ten people allocated eighteen dollars or more each to this benefit.

In addition, employees were asked what benefit they were willing to spend their own money on obtaining. The number of responses follows:

Employee Life Insurance	19
Additional Life Insurance	16
Dependant Life Insurance	19
AD&D	13
Travel Insurance	7
Vision Benefits	21
Eyeglasses Discount Insurance	21
Time Away from Work	12
Employee Dental Insurance	9
Dependant Dental Insurance	4
Day Care Center	20
Employee Health Insurance	7
Dependant Health Insurance	13
Pension Plan	16
Gainsharing	14
Short-Term Disability Insurance	14
Long-Term Disability Insurance	13
Cash	0
Employee Assistance Plan	6
Prescription Drug Plan	12

Five employees indicated they desired some type of 401(K) or IRA plan. Seventy-nine employees indicated no benefit for which they would spend their own money. Two employees added tuition assistance to the list.

Write-in Responses

Of the 110 written comments received, only 7 were perceived to be negative. Others, although sometimes critical, were viewed as positive and constructive. However, as with any written comments, they have more meaning when read by management accountable for the area from which they were generated.

Of the groups for which results were reported, levels of significance were calculated to determine when a reported group significantly differed from the balance of employees. Complete charts of these results are included with the statistics. However, some general observations can be made.

Not surprisingly, Executive Management was the most significantly positive, and Professionals the most negative. Employees who have been with the company three to five years were the most negative compared with other groups, and employees with a year or less of service were the most positive. Of the departments, Marketing and Health Services were the most positive and Administration and Finance were the most negative.

There were a number of questions included in the survey on total quality management. However, not knowing the details of that program, these will have to be reviewed individually by the organization to assess their significance. Likewise, since there was no previous history of Recognition, it is somewhat difficult to supply a comparison.

Analysis

In many ways, this year's survey shows a marked improvement from the previous one. However, there are still some areas with which the company should be concerned. The following represents our overall analysis within each of the dimensions.

Overall Company

In all comparable questions, responses improved this year. This is particularly interesting because, since the last survey, fifty-eight employees have been added. (At least that is the number indicated by the two survey populations.) The company continues to be seen as a positive place to work by its employees.

Company Policies

Company Policies received a more positive reaction this year. This was supported by information obtained in the focus groups. A typical quote was:

> HR policies have certainly improved the last year.

However, there is still a problem, although slightly less severe, of unequal administration between and within departments. This was supported by every focus group. However, based on the focus groups' inputs, the policies that seem to be causing the most problems are those that have to do with time away from work and dress codes—areas in which the supervisor is provided more leniency for interpretation than in other areas. The key word in every focus group was "favoritism"—different employees being treated differently by the same supervisor.

Although the focus groups mentioned differences between departments, they were primarily concerned with differences within departments.

Job Performance

After a dip in last year's survey, this has again picked up. Employees seem to like their jobs. They like what they are doing, and they feel they are making a significant contribution. However, our interpretation of the focus groups' inputs and the comments under Training and Development and Opportunity to Advance was that this improvement may be short-lived. Employees are looking for opportunities to move ahead and are somewhat concerned as to whether or not they will discover them at the company.

To some extent, this may be a result of lack of work experience. A large portion of the company's workforce is young and seemingly working their first jobs. These individuals lack comparisons other than family life, part-time jobs, and prior schooling. Several indicated a less-than-realistic perception of growth within an organization.

Fairness and Responsibility

This was a new dimension. In prior years, the closest dimension, surveyed was Equal Treatment, so it is somewhat difficult to make direct comparisons. From the questions that can be compared, there appears to be an improvement in this area. Also, the focus groups indicated a perception that employees were generally treated very fairly at the company. When employees were perceived as not being treated fairly, it had to do with favoritism and not such things as sex, race, or age.

Three of the four focus groups discussed college degrees. This came up when reviewing opportunities for advancement. Employees felt that the company favors external degree people over existing employees. They saw this as often unfair and unnecessary, so if there is any feeling of unfair treatment, it is toward employees not possessing college degrees.

Training and Development

Training and Development improved this year. It is still in need of attention, but employees felt that since the last survey the company has become serious about providing training and development opportunities. Both in the focus groups and on the written response sheets.

In the focus groups, there was some concern that the training programs offered are not practical enough and they need to include more devices or techniques for direct application to jobs.

There was a concern expressed that training within departments for specific job duties is not proceduralized or formalized. It was "catch-as-catch-can." They felt work should be done to standardize such training.

Job Security

Responses to the key Job Security question showed a decline in satisfaction, but that is not surprising given external economic circumstances and related media coverage. The other results of the survey in this dimension are the most positive that we've seen the past year. Employees feel the company is one of the few organizations that has been able to provide stable employment during the much-publicized recession.

Supervision

Supervision, for another year, remains relatively unchanged. However, there was a definite increase in employees' perceptions of their supervisor's human relations skills. In the focus groups, they indicated this was due to the training and development that has been provided.

Change

Change is a concern to employees. They feel there is too much of it, and they do not feel it has been adequately handled. Some of this relates to the quality customer service program. All of the focus groups indicated that although they are very positive about the approach, they do not see it being correctly implemented. If they are correct, the company is getting some backlash for introducing a program but not proceeding with it in a perceived positive fashion.

Employees also expressed concern that they are not involved in change. Change is forced on them with little consideration for their needs or ideas. One employee said:

> It just seems to me if you're going to change someone's job, you might ask that person first for his or her ideas.

Employees are also concerned about the amount of organizational change—particularly in upper management. Over the past year or so, there has been a great deal of movement. This leads to some uncertainty and concern.

Generally, employees recognize that the world is changing and changing fast. They are willing to accept this, but the company needs to concentrate on how it communicates change and how it involves employees in decisions about change.

Communication

Communication suffered a great drop in positive responses in this year's survey. Most of this reaction appears to be based on the quality customer service program and the amount of change. These have both been touched on already, and comments are included later in this analysis.

To some extent, the employees in the focus groups indicated that the avenues of communication are improving. They seem to feel their immediate supervisor is now a better source of information than in the past, and they speak positively about the employee newsletter. Their complaints have more to do with a "lack" of communication.

This was such a negative reaction that the company needs to give this area immediate attention.

Compensation

Compensation has somewhat improved. The 34 percent positive response is typical in employee surveys for this dimension. Even when pleased, employees rarely seem to respond too positively. We have always interpreted this as a tendency not to say, "I'm getting paid more than I should be."

A negative in this area was the dip in the positive responses of the relationship between performance and pay. The focus groups did not explain the reason for this, other than that there is a relatively negative reaction to the gainsharing program. Perhaps, this is due to its newness and their lack of experience with it.

Benefits

Satisfaction with benefits remains remarkably high. Employees are very pleased with their benefit program. There is little to do here except possibly improve eyeglasses benefits.

If the laws are changed and it is possible to offer employees some type of 401(k), that will be greeted very positively. Unfortunately, many still do not understand why this is not provided.

Another area of concern has already been mentioned—gainsharing. Employees do not seem to understand this program, and considerable concern was expressed regarding the elimination of the holiday bonus.

On the written response sheet, the questions that were asked regarding the allocation of money for benefits were a method to examine the possibility of flexible benefits. It is our interpretation that flexible benefits would provide no advantage to the company or the employees at this point. We feel it would be a rather expensive installation activity that would be seen negatively.

Department Procedures

Unfortunately, since the questions in this dimension were changed so greatly, the only one that allowed comparison with prior years referred to department organization. However, the feeling gained in the focus groups was that the departments are perceived to be running pretty well, but some attention needs to be given to both Finance and Administration. If the information received is correct, these have both undergone major top management changes the past year, and this may be some of the reason for concern. Here, the written comments should prove of great assistance.

Opportunity for Advancement

Responses to the two key questions here tended to contradict each other. Rating of long-term career potential has dropped, but opportunity to move ahead in the company has somewhat increased. This was explored during the focus groups, and our interpretation is that employees feel that opportunities now exist within the company, but they do not believe they will be the recipients of these opportunities. This ties back to some of the remarks made about training and particularly the concern for hiring of external people with college degrees for the best jobs.

The focus groups also expressed a good deal of concern with the job-posting program. They felt it was an excellent program to provide opportunities for employees. However, they indicated situations in which they were denied interviews or told they did not have the degree necessary for the job. Potentially, this could be a problem, and we might want to examine offering some type of career path development training. Also, this might be an area in which to consider a survey to determine exactly what it is people want—that is, where do they want to go.

Executive Management

Executive Management's positive evaluation dropped this year. However, of real interest is the fact that their evaluation of themselves dropped. It is a very small group. The group has several new members and, if our memory is correct, a couple of its members declined to participate in last year's survey. In any event, there appears to be the basis for an interesting discussion at a Quality Council meeting about executive management's responses to this year's employee opinion survey questions.

Quality Customer Service

As already mentioned, we are unfamiliar with the details of the company's total quality management program, and this is a relatively new dimension for us to measure. To date, companies, including those with total quality management programs, have been averaging somewhere in the high 60 percent for positive responses, so the 72 percent is quite positive.

In reviewing the individual items, our concern was the somewhat low positive responses of executives. Generally, they are the most positive when such a program is being implemented. Also, in answer to the question, What is your level of understanding of quality customer service?—only 43 percent of employees responded favorably. Fifty-six percent indicated they had too little information.

All of the customer service questions in this dimension and those scattered through other dimensions need to be collected and examined by the appropriate people. Our overall feeling is that employees see it as an excellent program, and, assuming it follows typical approaches, it is probably a program that will solve many of the employees' concerns such as Change and Communication. At this time, employees feel it is something that was started and is now not being properly or completely implemented. One employee said:

> I went to that big party out in the tent. I was really enthused, and I haven't heard another word about it since.

Recognition

Recognition is another new dimension this year. There were no prior years with which to compare it. Comparing it with other organizations in which we surveyed such a dimension, it was on the low positive side. Generally, we expect to receive positive responses in the low 60 percentile. Here again, we think these questions and the written comments need to be examined by individual departments.

The focus groups talked a good deal about recognition. They felt that there is a lack of overall company recognition. They indicated the only program they know about is Employee of the Season. They want more recognition but not necessarily anything elaborate.

Their major concern, for those who were concerned, was with individual supervisors. They are looking for the kind word, the job well done, and the pat on the back. Possibly these will come with the continued management training that is occurring.

Conclusions

The company has recaptured some of the ground it appeared to have lost in its last employee opinion survey. The major areas of concern at that time have shown a turn upward. This is particularly remarkable with the number of new employees who have been added. However, the older employees seem to be somewhat less positive.

Human resource issues received a far more positive response this year, and Training and Development and Company Policies were seen as improving. Change and Communication have both declined significantly.

As mentioned under Quality Customer Service, the program is probably the answer to many of the indicated problems, but it has to be seen as more than a temporary activity. Also, to many employees, it is viewed as a process—a system—rather than a "way of community life." It needs to be seen as having meaning for employees as well as the company. On the basis of the survey, there's probably no single activity that can assist the company more than the proper implementation of this program.

Since one of the motivations for conducting an employee opinion survey is to identify areas that need attention, a good deal of this report has focused on such comments. However, this year's employee opinion survey results need to be put in an overall perspective. Of all the surveys we have conducted the past three years, this year's results are by far the most positive. In our opinion, the company employs a group of positive and dedicated people. They like their company and their jobs. They want to see the company grow, and they want to grow and develop with it. At this point their comments and concerns are very constructive.

Second Report

The second report is from a southern manufacturing company. The Company is over fifty years old. Its service and production personnel are unionized. The report along with all statistics was delivered to the senior management group by the consultant who conducted and tabulated the survey.

Introduction

During the first two weeks of December, an employee opinion survey was conducted with all employees. It was administered on site by representatives of the Company's survey consulting firm to approximately 1,612 employees. An additional 214 employees completed the survey the third week of December and mailed their results directly to the consulting firm. In total, 1,826 completed surveys were received and analyzed. An additional 4 surveys arrived too late for the computer analysis.

During January, fifty-two employees participated in five focus group discussions based on the initial survey results, and 859 (47 percent of those participating in the survey) provided written responses to a follow-up survey.

The survey was similar in design to a previous one conducted one year ago in the spring. However, several revisions were made:

Two of the dimensions used in the earlier survey were subdivided to provide more meaningful information.

A quality customer service dimension was added.

The number of questions requiring written responses was increased.

Questions regarding the use of the last survey's results were added.

Survey Objectives

To reinforce the Company's concerns of the opinions of its employees.

To further improve two-way communication between the Company and its employees.

To identify current employee perceptions regarding key elements and conditions of their employment.

To identify and implement actions to increase effective management practices.

To identify employee perceptions regarding the use of results from the last opinion survey.

To identify employee perceptions regarding the Company's concern for quality customer service.

To identify changes in employee perceptions since the last employee opinion survey.

Methodology

The survey was administered and focus groups conducted by representatives of the company's survey consulting firm at all major facilities of the Company. Surveys to be mailed directly to the consulting firm were provided for those employees who did not attend one of the on-site sessions.

The survey consisted of 113 multiple-choice questions and 10 questions requiring written responses. The majority of multiple-choice responses were analyzed in fourteen work-related dimensions.

Dimensions

Overall Company

Company Policies

Job Performance

Department Procedures

Immediate Supervision

Job Security

Pay and Benefits

Communication

Executive Management

Equal Treatment

Opportunity to Advance

Change

Training

Quality Customer Service

Response Categories

For each multiple-choice question, there were five possible responses:

Strongly Positive

Positive

Neutral

Negative

Strongly Negative

For reporting purposes, these were reduced to three categories:

Favorable (Strongly Positive and Positive)

Neutral

Unfavorable (Strongly Negative and Negative)

Results are reported as a percentage of the employees responding. Since sometimes employees did not answer a specific question and at other times employees provided two or more answers to a question, percentages always do not total 100 percent.

Survey Demographics

Department

Employee Group

Gender

Education

Age

Race

Seniority

Length of Service

Provided Reports

Complete Company report including all subgroups and copies of written responses

Reports by executives with requested subdivisions and employee's written responses for each executive's area of accountability

Summary report and analysis to management from the consulting firm—similar to one provided with the last survey as a basis for communication to employees

Results

Total employees completing questionnaires	1,826
Executive Management	22
Director/Management	115
Supervisor/Foremen	195
Management Professionals/Management Clerical	350
Union	994
Unidentified	150

Gender

Male	1,229
Female	465
Unidentified	132

Race

African-American	452
White	1,142
Other Races	95
Unidentified	137

Tenure

Less than one year	31
One year to five years	274
Five years to fifteen years	547
Fifteen years or more	857
Unidentified	117

Age

Twenty-four years and younger	54
Twenty-five years to thirty-four years	131
Thirty-five years to forty-nine years	923
50 years and older	321
Unidentified	397

By Vice President Group

Vice President A	446
Plant 1	45
Plant 2	76
Plant 3	79
Plant 4	71
Suboffice	175
Vice President B	73
Vice President C	87
Marketing/Sales	32
Balance	55
Vice President D	179
Vice President E	139
Vice President F	270
Building and Special Services	66
Information Systems and Services	96
Operation Services	85
Balance	23
Vice President G	29
Vice President H	293
Maintenance	50
Engineering	3
Inventory Control	78
Appliance Repair	74
Telephone and Customer Services	56
Balance	42
Vice President I	36
Vice President J	16
Vice President K	37
Vice President L	33
Unidentified	188

Favorable Responses Compared With Similar Companies

Dimension	Company	Other Companies
Overall Company	39 %	38 %
Company Policies	30 %	48 %
Job Performance	67 %	64 %
Department Procedures	38 %	51 %
Immediate Supervision	47 %	52 %
Job Security	57 %	60 %
Pay and Benefits	47 %	35 %
Communication	36 %	32 %
Executive Management	40 %	46 %
Equal Treatment	47 %	57 %
Opportunity to Advance	32 %	39 %
Change	18 %	53 %
Training	36 %	44 %
Quality Customer Service		
Overall Change Since 1987	8.7 %	(10.1 %)

Last Survey and This Survey

Dimension	Last Year	This Year	Change
Overall Company	33 %	39 %	2 %
Company Policies	N/A	30 %	N/A
Job Performance	49 %	67 %	3 %
Department Procedures	N/A	38 %	N/A
Immediate Supervision	44 %	47 %	3 %
Job Security	50 %	57 %	7 %
Pay and Benefits	53 %	47 %	(6 %)
Communication	29 %	36 %	7 %
Executive Management	38 %	40 %	2 %
Equal Treatment	35 %	47 %	5 %
Opportunity to Advance	N/A	32 %	N/A
Change	16 %	18 %	2 %
Training	37 %	36 %	(1 %)
Quality Customer Service	N/A	57 %	N/A

Overall Comments

There is a positive trend in the Company survey results since the last survey, but a negative trend compared to results from other companies.

The decrease in Pay and Benefits appears to be a reaction to general economic conditions and employee's perceptions that executive management has received a more significant compensation increase than the balance of employees.

Company Policies are viewed as positive, but inconsistent department administration still is viewed as negative.

Although there were a number of positive actions initiated as the result of the last survey, employees do not perceive the connections. This had a somewhat negative impact on responses.

Training is seen as an area in which improvement was promised but not implemented.

There have been major increases in positive responses among employee groups.

There are less differences between employee groups.

The most significant negative groups were:

- Union Employees
- Five to fifteen years of service
- Twenty-five- to thirty-four-year-olds
- Vice President A's Departments
- Vice President H's Departments

It is important to note that Vice President A's department and Vice President H's department have a substantially high number of organized workers, and that is the primary reason for the negative status.

Quality Customer Service is a positive objective that requires additional implementation, but employees fail to see a personal benefit from it.

The most positive groups were:

- ❑ Executive Management
- ❑ Director/Management
- ❑ Supervisor/Foremen
- ❑ African-American
- ❑ Less than one year of tenure
- ❑ Age fifty years or older
- ❑ Vice President F's Departments

Quality Customer Service

Since a quality customer service program was introduced following the previous survey, ten questions were created regarding that program:

Anticipated favorable response for entire Company	43 %
Actual favorable response for entire Company	57.5%

Companywide positive responses to specific quality customer service questions:

The Company is concerned with satisfying our customers.	84%
My Department is concerned with satisfying our customers.	81%
Providing quality service has a positive impact on business.	92%
How do you rate the Company's concern for satisfying our customers?	68%

Quality customer service positive responses by area:

Vice President A	56.5%
Vice President B	52.8%
Vice President C	52.4%
Vice President D	61.0%

Vice President E	58.2%
Vice President F	64.3%
Vice President G	50.7%
Vice President H	48.3%
Vice President I	53.5%
Vice President J	65.2%
Vice President K	64.5%
Vice President L	47.4%
Unidentified	61.2%

Quality Service Comments

Employees recognize the relationship between quality customer service and Company success.

Employees do not perceive a relationship between providing quality customer service and individual rewards.

Employees do not feel all of their ideas are taken into consideration for the improvement of quality.

Company Satisfaction

A new comparison measure initiated this year is a company satisfaction index. It consists of a total score that represents the favorable responses in questions 91 through 103, dealing with the total Company.

The average satisfaction index received from other companies' surveys has been 36.4 percent.

The overall company satisfaction index reported by this survey is 49.1 percent.

Use of the Results from the Last Survey

Item	Favorable	Neutral	Unfavorable
How well were the results of the last survey used by the Company?	16%	47%	37%
How well do you feel the results of the last opinion survey reflected your understanding as to the conditions of the Company?	25%	47%	27%
How well were the results of the last opinion survey communicated to employees?	27%	37%	36%
How well do you feel the results of the last employee opinion survey were used to improve conditions at the Company?	16%	37%	47%

Comments on Actions Taken Since the Last Survey

Few actions are perceived to have occurred as a result of the last survey. Employees recognize some actions that occurred but do not connect them to the results of the last survey.

Employees are generally positive about the actions that have occurred.

Employees want the Company to respond positively to the survey with follow-up actions.

Employees want greater quality of communication and less quantity of communication.

Employees recognize the need for change but hope it will be less in the coming years. Employees feel there is a larger than necessary gap between executive management and the balance of the company.

Nonmanagement employees feel they are bearing the brunt of the current economic situation while executive management is continuing to be rewarded.

There is a great desire for an improvement in the training promised and offered.

There is a desire for a consistency in the administration of Company policies.

Suggested Action Steps

Prepare a Report to Employees.

Present the results to the senior management group, distribute individual reports to them, and prepare an Employee Opinion Survey results feedback plan.

Make a presentation to all management employees.

Hold departmental meetings with employees to distribute their Report to Employees, answer questions, and identify actions that can be taken within the department.

Feed back action steps to senior management.

Follow up on action steps.

Commit to a specific date (the spring is recommended) for conducting the next Employee Opinion Survey.

Provide regular (every six months) reports of implementation of actions.

SAMPLE REPORTS FOR EMPLOYEES

It is better to know some of the questions than all of the answers.

JAMES THURBER

(QUOTED BY ROBERT W. KENT, "MICROECONOMICS," *Money Talks*, 1985)

This chapter contains two sample reports. The first is a report for a Midwest financial services firm. It was delivered as a special edition of the employee newsletter and followed up with department meetings. Management's action plans for five dimensions were included.

A Report to All Employees of Our Annual Employee Opinion Survey

In September, nearly 2,000 of our employees participated in our third Employees' Views opinion survey. That was more than 90 percent of employees, and as in the past, we are pleased to report to all employees the results of that survey.

Each survey produces results with their own characteristics. Since we have conducted past surveys, we were able to use this year's survey results to measure the progress made since the previous ones. In addition, the survey provided management information that can be used to continue our commitment to make our company the best place to work in the country.

The surveys were administered by members of our human resources department and on completion were sent directly to an external firm for tabulation. The questions were grouped into seventeen dimensions. Sixteen of those dimensions were similar to those in past surveys. The new dimension related to our use of such surveys and their results. The surveys and written comments were tabulated and reported back anonymously by the external firm. It then destroyed all of the original survey forms.

Below is a summary table of responses. Questions on the survey asked you to indicate how important each dimension was to you. The table lists the dimensions in your descending order of importance. The percent of favorable responses is shown for each dimension along with the percentages from the two previous surveys.

There are five dimensions that appear to be of broad concern to our employees: Compensation, Career Development, Performance Evaluation, Training, and Communication. The following are the results of management's review of these dimensions and the actions we will undertake.

Compensation

Although favorable responses have improved each year, there are still concerns with this dimension of employment. Your responses to the individual questions indicate that employees have the impression that pay levels do not provide an adequate differential between new employees and more experienced ones in similar jobs. There were also comments that performance is not adequately recognized.

Employees seem to feel the total of benefits and compensation is competitive, but they are not fully satisfied with the mix of ele-

Dimension	This Year's Favorable Responses	Last Year's Favorable Responses	Two Years Ago's Favorable Responses
Job Security	73	66	60
Benefits	87	80	70
Compensation	43	39	32
Career Development	59	52	48
Performance Evaluation	53	53	48
Job Satisfaction	67	62	64
Supervision	65	63	65
Working Relationships	75	72	70
Polices & Procedures	72	72	62
Environment	63	60	62
Management	63	65	60
Training	58	60	55
Communications	56	51	45
Company Image	88	77	68
Efficiency	61	61	61
Quality	88	84	82
Reaction to survey	77	NA	NA

ments. They feel it is not appropriate for all employees and there needs to be a more flexible approach.

Action Plans

We have retained a consulting firm to conduct a total review of our compensation program. This will occur during the next four months, and a report will be delivered by March 1.

The review's objective is to assess all elements of our compensation program in terms of equity issues and competitiveness.

When the review is completed, its results along with any required action will be communicated to you.

Career Development

Actually, we looked at three dimensions that are related: Career Development, Performance Evaluation, and Training. All three had relatively low favorable responses. One of the key issues in these areas concerned our job-posting program. Apparently, many of you do not feel it is an efficient and fair way of communicating job opportunities.

A second concern was the amount of training for current employees. You feel training for new employees is adequate, but training for employees moving to other jobs and in preparation for possible promotion requires improvement.

A number of you feel the performance evaluation program concentrates on compensation adjustments and ignores development for the future.

Action Plans

Beginning next month, our human resources department will conduct a series of focus groups to evaluate the job-posting program to determine what revisions are required to meet employee needs. Simultaneously, an assessment of our existing training will be conducted to evaluate the effectiveness of existing training and the relationship of training offered to job requirements. Finally, sessions will be held with all management to stress the importance of career development as a part of the performance evaluation program.

We hope these three initiatives will result in improvements in all three dimensions that will become apparent at our next survey.

Communication

There has been improvement in favorable response to communication over the past three years, but it is still below where it should be. A number of initiatives have been created and implemented based on survey results. There is more direct communication with employees than there was in past, but the grapevine continues to function. Unfortunately, it often communicates misinformation.

We interpreted this year's survey as requesting more face-to-face communication between management and employees, particularly with respect to important company and job information. Also, the need for timely communication was often mentioned.

Action Plans

We will continue to review our communication and investigate additional ways of involving all of us. As a start, each supervisor will be given a copy of the survey results for her department. A meeting will be held with all department employees to review those results and develop any action plans for areas under your control. These meetings will then be held quarterly to review progress and establish an ongoing dialogue.

Conclusion

The survey results were encouraging, but all of us still face the challenge of making our company the very best place to work. In four short years, we have seen significant improvements resulting from these surveys, yet there is still much to do. Your management is committed to learning from these surveys and taking action as needed. We want to always be the employer of choice.

Manufacturing Company Report

The following is a report written to all employees of a southeastern manufacturing company. It was signed by the company's president and mailed to each employee at home. It addresses each dimension, first reporting survey results and then a company response. This was the second employee opinion survey conducted by this company.

As with the previous example, it appears as used by the company as a base for two-way communication.

A Report to Employees of the Annual Employee Opinion Survey

Overall Company Survey Results

The key question in this area was "All in all, how do you rate our company as a place to work compared with other companies you know about?" Sixty-six percent of employees responded favorably to this question. In the previous year's survey, 63 percent responded favorably. Only 5 percent responded negatively to this question.

Company Response

We were quite pleased last year to learn that 63 percent of our employees found our company to be a good place to work, so the fact that number has increased to 66 percent this year is even more rewarding. We want to be a company all of us are proud to be associated with, and that will only occur as we continue to work together.

Only 5 percent of employees responding to this question did so in a negative way. However, even that low number is disappointing to us. We hope, by the time of the next survey, that 5 percent also will see our company as an excellent place to work.

You might be interested in knowing that this number of favorable responses is significantly stronger than those received to the same question at companies similar to ours. Those averaged favorable responses of only 5 percent.

Company Policies Survey Results

Favorable responses regarding the quality of company personnel policies were similar to those from last year's survey. In both surveys, 56 percent of employees felt that overall company policies were typical or better than typical. However, 69 percent of you felt that policies were administered inconsistently in different departments. Specific mention was made of the sick leave policy.

Company Response

This was a disappointing response. Last year, I stated that the consistent administration of personnel policies is a company goal and necessity, and I pledged that steps would be taken to eliminate the problem. Apparently, those steps have not been enough.

I have asked the vice president of human resources to review the written responses to the survey. Within the next two months, he will summarize those results and report them to the senior management group. At that point, we will take the necessary steps to ensure that company policies are indeed administered equitably within all departments except where specific conditions require differences. Let us hope that by the time of the next survey, this will be an area in which the vast majority of you respond positively.

Job Performance Survey Results

Sixty-seven percent of employees like their jobs, 84 percent of them know the results expected, 67 percent report their work gives them a feeling of accomplishment, and 83 percent feel positively about the work they are performing. These are extremely high statistics, and they represent substantial increases in favorable responses since the last survey.

Company Response

We think this is a very positive result. Most of us spend a good portion of our waking hours on our jobs. Liking them and liking the company for which we work are rewarding conditions for most of us. It gives us the feeling of making significant contributions.

Your positive feelings about the company and your jobs provide a strong base. It is a base on which we can build and grow to fulfilling our individual and collective missions and visions.

Immediate Supervision Survey Results

This is another area in which favorable responses have somewhat increased since the last survey. In the previous survey, 44 percent of employees responded positively. This year, 47 percent responded positively. In analyzing written responses, in focus groups, and in responses to individual questions, it became apparent that the concern about the unequal administration of policies is having an impact.

Company Response

As a result of survey comments, a new training program for supervisors and managers was introduced following the last survey. This program was designed to assist our supervisors and managers to become as effective in their human relations as they are in the technical aspects of their jobs. We hope your increased favorable responses in this area seem to be somewhat the result of that program. However, your concern about the administration of policies seems to be having an impact in several areas.

Following the last survey, we indicated that we were going to make an effort to ensure your supervisor was a key element in the formal communication process. We think that has been somewhat accomplished, but our efforts this year will be to continue to improve that process. In fact, you are actually receiving the results of this survey from your supervisor.

Department Procedures Survey Results

Department Procedures is a somewhat difficult dimension for which to provide comparison information. Collectively, all of the questions in this area produced only a 38 percent favorable response. That is somewhat lower than responses in this dimension from other companies we have surveyed, and since it was not a separate dimension in the last survey, there is no comparison of the changes that may have occurred.

There are major differences between the favorable results from individual departments. Again, this seems to be somewhat a result of the administration of policies, but there are also some key areas of concern in individual departments. Individual managers need to review the statistical results along with the written responses and identify the necessary actions that need to take place.

Company Response

In four dimensions, Company Policies, Job Performance, Immediate Supervisor, and Department Procedures, the impact of how company policies are administered was mentioned.

This was a concern in the last survey, and although there have been some improvements made, apparently employees do not feel that enough has occurred. This indicates that we need to take significant action in this area. As already mentioned, the vice president of human resources has been asked to look into the specifics of this situation and prepare a report within the next two months.

This is an area to which you and your supervisor or manager should be giving some thought. It may be that action steps need to be developed within individual departments.

Job Security Survey Results

Overall, the favorable responses in this dimension increased from 50 percent last year to 57 percent this year. Written responses and focus group responses indicated that there was recognition of the company's need to better control expenses and reduce the number of employees in order to remain competitive, but it was expressed that the company was doing this in a fair and equitable way.

Company Response

We were surprised that job security was as favorable as it was. We felt that given the recent reduction in force, employees might be somewhat insecure about their positions. However, feelings of job security have actually increased. Employees seem to feel that although it was necessary to reduce the number of positions in the company, management did it in a fair and equitable way, so there should now be no concern about losing a job. The only negative impact seems to be with opportunities to advance.

In that dimension, employees still feel there are opportunities within the company, but they do not believe that they are going to be made available to them. They see the reduction in force size as a limiting factor. They also see what they believe to be the lack of training for advancement as a limiting factor.

Opportunity to Advance Survey Results

Overall, 32 percent of employees responded favorably to questions in this dimension, but results for the dimension cannot be compared to last year's survey since the dimension was not included in that survey. Favorable results were somewhat lower than those received from other companies responding to questions on a similar survey.

Last year, 18 percent of the employees responded favorably with respect to the number of opportunities for their advancement, but this year, only 13 percent responded favorably. However, 56 percent responded favorably with respect to the number of opportunities that will probably develop within the company.

Company Response

In the previous dimension, Job Security, I made comments regarding opportunities to advance and their relationship to job security. The report in this dimension provides statistical evidence of how you feel and supports the comments in job security.

The reduction in force somewhat eliminated the immediate opportunities for advancement, since the number of positions were reduced. However, you are correct in believing that in the long run there will be more opportunities. It is certainly our belief, as we move forward in our efforts to improve the quality of our work and introduce new services, that the company will grow.

Pay and Benefits Survey Results

This was one of two areas in which favorable responses decreased since the last survey. In the previous survey, 56 percent of employees responded favorably to questions in this dimension. This year, only 47 percent responded favorably. Looking at specific questions, favorable responses regarding pay decreased from 77 percent to 49 percent, and favorable responses to benefit questions decreased from 71 percent to 65 percent.

Company Response

We were somewhat surprised with the low perceptions of pay and benefits.

We are continually conducting surveys to determine the relationships of our pay and benefits with those of other companies, and the results of those surveys indicate that our pay generally is equal to or higher than that in similar jobs at other companies. Perhaps this was more of a reflection of the times. Certainly, bad economic news was somewhat affecting us all.

Whatever the case, we will continue to conduct pay and benefit surveys. It is our policy to pay a competitive wage and provide competitive benefits. We will be conducting a survey of pay and benefits next month, and the results of that survey will be made available to all employees.

With respect to our organized employees, pay and benefits are a subject of collective bargaining, so they must be evaluated in the context of a total collective bargaining agreement.

In the area of benefits, there was some desire indicated for expansion of dental and health benefits, the addition of an eyeglass program, and additional retirement benefits. The human resources department has been asked to examine these areas—specifically comments in these areas. We want to determine exactly what is being said and then review the implications to our cost situation and our total benefit package of considering such options.

Communication Survey Results

Favorable responses to communication significantly increased, from 29 percent to 36 percent. That is a 7 percent increase, and the 36 percent is higher than similar surveys conducted at other companies.

Company Response

Communication has definitely improved, but there may be a bit of a backlash. In the written responses, there was a concern of quantity over quality. Perhaps there needs to be a coordination of communication media such as newsletters.

The reorganization of our communication department is a step in the right direction, and they are going to be reviewing all employee communication media. We want to ensure communication is accurate and delivered in the best possible fashion.

You still feel you do not receive your communication through the right sources. You still want your supervisor to be the vital key in the communication link, and we want that too. That is one reason the results of this survey are being communicated to you by your supervisor.

The Employee Opinion Survey itself is a key communication, and I will have more things to say about it and overall communication.

Executive Management Survey Results

The employees' favorable responses to executive management increased from 38 percent to 40 percent. However, a gap still exists between the perceptions of executive management and other employees. Particularly cited was the executive option program recently announced in the company's report to stockholders, but it is our interpretation that the concern here was more for the way the program was handled and communicated than the realities of it. Also, there was an indication in the written responses that it did not seem appropriate at the time the reduction in force was occurring.

Company Response

We are pleased that there is an improvement in your favorable responses to executive management, but we are disappointed the favorable responses were not higher. When we examined individual questions, we see that you feel more positively about how executive management views the customers, and we think that is important. However, we also want you to feel positively about executive management's concern for the employee.

You are probably right with respect to the executive option program. Since most of you are also stockholders, we probably should have let you know in another fashion what was being considered, but you must note that the program was recommended and approved by the company's board of directors. That board of directors represents you—the stockholders. You elected them, and therefore you indirectly vote on such proposals.

We heard you. We need to do a better job of communicating, and we need to do a better job of letting you know where things stand. We need to do a better job of communicating to you the reasons for decisions.

Equal Treatment Survey Results

Equal treatment favorable responses increased significantly. Last year there was a 35 percent favorable response. This year there was a 47 percent favorable response. Moreover, there were fewer perceptions of specific unequal treatment within the organization.

Company Response

At the conclusion of the last survey, I reaffirmed the company's strong commitment to equal employment opportunity, and I stated that policy is continually monitored to ensure that no one is discriminated against due to age, sex, race, physical handicap, marital status, religion, national origin, or veteran status. However, we did take a closer look at it to ensure that our employees were being treated equally, and we are quite confident they are.

Discrimination will never be tolerated at our company. If, at any time, you believe it has occurred, you should immediately bring it to the attention of your equal employment opportunity manager or your supervisor. This is an area in which I hope we will continue to see favorable responses increase.

Change Survey Results

Change's favorable responses have shown an improvement. They increased from 16 percent to 18 percent. Employee responses to individual questions and written comments indicate that employees are still unhappy with the amount of change, but they recognize to a large extent it is not under anyone's control. However, they do feel that the company is doing a better job of managing that change.

Company Response

Change is still a problem. Our economy and our country are experiencing many negative events, and these external factors affect us. All we can do is plan and manage such change as best we can, so we are pleased you feel we are doing better at it.

Training Survey Results

Training is the second dimension in which there was a decrease in favorable responses since the last survey. It has gone from 37 percent to 31 percent. The 37 percent is significantly lower than the favorable responses for similar surveys conducted at other companies.

Company Response

Training appears to be a concern to all of our employees, and we have closely examined your written responses and answers to individual questions. We think that one of the problems is that employees are unaware of some of the steps taken following the last survey.

At the conclusion of that survey, I promised that our training department would conduct an analysis of the training being offered as well as an employee training needs study. Those things occurred, but I don't think we communicated the results to you in an effective fashion.

One of the actions identified by the training needs analysis was that our supervisors and managers needed additional training. That need also was reflected in a number of your responses in the last survey, so the first order of business was to institute such a training program. That program was initiated, and 84 percent of our supervisors and managers have participated in that training.

I have asked our training department to again look at this whole area and to publish communication to all of you within the next three months that indicates what training is currently available. Then, we will keep this updated, so you always will be aware of what opportunities for training exist within the company.

Quality Customer Service Survey Results

This was a new dimension this year. In fact, it is a relatively new dimension for most companies conducting similar surveys. Based on the results of other companies, we anticipated a 47 percent favorable response in this dimension. The actual favorable response was 53 percent.

In examining written responses and answers to individual questions, it became apparent that employees are quite favorably inclined to providing quality customer service. However, they express concern for the relationship between their known success and such an effort.

Company Response

We are very pleased to discover that our employees look favorably on providing quality customer service. We all know that there are many alternatives to the product and service we provide, and we strongly believe that what will make the difference is the quality of our product and the quality of our service.

In the long run, providing a quality service and product are the things that will make us a success, and the success of this company is directly related to your individual success. As the company grows and prospers, so will you, but perhaps we need to spend more time with you to establish this relationship.

As you are aware, there are many efforts under way within the company in all departments to introduce our approach to quality customer service. If you and your department are not already involved, you will be shortly. This should do much to provide you with the information you need in this area, but as the year goes on, I think you are going to discover that quality customer service is one of the keys to our individual and collective success.

Summary

There were many things about the results of this year's Employee Opinion Survey that pleased us. While the favorable results from most companies decreased an average of 10 percent, ours increased an average of almost 9 percent. In negative economic times, our employees gained a more favorable opinion of their company and their working conditions.

In most of those areas where there still appears to be a need for improvement, the specific reasons were relatively well identified. There are things on which we can take action. In other instances, our feeling is that we just need to do a better job of communicating. We feel that if we do that, you will better understand the decisions that have been made.

Since this was the second survey conducted, it included a series of questions regarding employee opinions of how the last survey results were used. The answers to these questions plus the information provided in the focus groups were somewhat disappointing. Many of you did not feel that anything resulted from the last survey. We feel a great deal resulted, and perhaps this is representative of our need to better communicate with you.

Let me provide you with a very specific example. In one of the focus groups, an employee stated that nothing was done to improve the quality of the supervisors and managers as a result of the last survey. The individual conducting the focus group mentioned the supervisor training program that was initiated after the last survey. The employees said yes, that it had happened, but it had nothing to do with the survey.

In fact, that program was a direct outgrowth of the last survey. As I indicated in the company's response to training, we heard what you said about the need for your supervisors and managers to become a more vital link in the communication process. We heard you say they needed improvement in their human resource abilities, and we took the necessary action. Again, perhaps we are not communicating as well as we should.

The Employee Opinion Survey is a part of our two-way communication process. To ensure that process is a continual one, I am going to be reporting back to you every six months on how we are progressing. I am going to be reporting what has happened as a result of the survey. I am going to be reporting to you other things that are occurring within the company that relate to the dimensions covered by this survey, and I am going to communicate how you are doing on your individual department action plans.

There is much that you and your individual departments can do to assist in making our company the type of company we wish it to be. I have asked each of your supervisors and managers to work with you. You should analyze the results of the survey written comments from your areas, and you should take the actions that are possible within your department.

We have scheduled the next survey to be conducted next year. Between then and now, I am pledging to you that we will do a better job of communicating with you. My firm belief is that we will show significant improvement in our future survey results.

I believe our company is an outstanding place at which to work. I believe we are a family of employees and a unique group working toward a common mission and vision. Together, we will continue to grow, prosper, and succeed.

CHAPTER 16

USING SUPERVISORS TO DELIVER RESULTS FOR TWO-WAY COMMUNICATION

Supervisor-subordinate relationships are undoubtedly among the oddest forms of human interactions. They are even stranger than kiwi birds at mating time.

JEFFERY G. ALLEN,
Surviving Corporate Downsizing

Employee opinion surveys provide an ideal basis for an effective two-way communication program between employees and management. It is initiated by management's desire for information from employees. Employees provide that information, and management reports the results to the employees. To an extent, two-way communication has already occurred, but it can easily be expanded. Department supervisors can play a critical role.

The Supervisor as the Key Communicator

Generally, the initial report of survey results is made to all employees by human resources or senior management. This provides a broad overview, but communication of survey results is more effective when it relates to each employee's situation. This can be accomplished through reporting results by department and by having the department supervisors deliver those results.

Supervisors (regardless of their titles) are the connection between the employees and management. In most companies, the supervisor is a key component of employees' satisfaction with their jobs and the company. Using the supervisor as a communicator of department survey results strengthens the supervisor's role and contributes to the development of department employees as a team, with the supervisor as its leader. Unfortunately, the supervisor is often bypassed.

In most surveys, there are responses that relate to areas that are best reviewed and improved at the department level. Department meetings can be an ongoing forum in which solutions can be developed, objectives for their implementation established, and follow-up discussions held. It produces an ideal basis for two-way dialogue between each supervisor and the employees reporting to the supervisor.

Notifying Employees

For a meeting to be successful, employees should be made aware of it in advance. In addition to being told when and where a meeting is to occur, they should also be told the objective of the meeting. This can be accomplished by memo, e-mail, or explained at a general meeting of all employees about the survey results.

If such supervisor-led meetings are typical, you will need relatively little advance explanation, but if this is an unusual occurrence in the company, the employees will need more detail. The important point is to make them fully aware of the meeting's purpose so they can prepare. This will lead to more effective communication.

The Communications Program

The first meeting in a two-way communication program of this type is a meeting of department employees conducted by the department supervisor. Its agenda is similar to the following:

>Overview of survey results for the company
>
>Questions and discussion of overall survey results
>
>Review of survey results that apply to the department
>
>Questions and discussion of department results
>
>Identification of areas of needed improvements that can be addressed at the department level
>
>Establishment of objectives of improvement based on survey results
>
>Assignments of responsibilities for implementing objectives

At the meeting, a time is established for a follow-up session to review progress in fulfilling the objectives.

Supervisor Preparation

The two crucial ingredients to making such a meeting a success are the use of department demographics and supervisor training.

Department Demographics

Obviously, the survey results cannot be reported by department unless such demographic identification is included as an element of the survey. This requires the decision to include such information to be made in advance of constructing the survey.

There is one caution, and that relates to departments with very few employees. Earlier we suggested that demographic information should not be collected for small departments. The best approach is to attempt to identify two or three small departments that are somewhat similar or related in their responsibilities and combine them. For example, assume you have three departments: shipping, inventory control, and packaging, and each has fewer than four employees. The departments are somewhat related, and in total they have fewer than 10 employees. You could combine them on the survey by identifying them for demographic selection as:

Shipping/inventory control/packaging departments

For meeting purposes, the employees from the three departments can be combined, and the three supervisors share in conducting the meeting.

Supervisor Training

In order for such meetings to be successful, the supervisors have to be provided with the survey information and a guide for conducting the meeting. Their training should be a group session that includes:

A review and discussion of overall survey results

A review and discussion of individual department results

A review and discussion of the department meeting agenda and approach

Practice in conducting the department meeting

Delivery of department survey results to each supervisor

Typically, a training session requires half a day (four hours). It should be conducted by someone familiar with meeting leadership techniques, and, in addition, someone should attend who understands all survey results.

In some companies, a member of the human resources department is scheduled to attend the first portion of each department meeting to answer survey-related questions. Once the survey results have been reviewed, the human resources person leaves, and the supervisor conducts the balance of the meeting.

Follow-Up

In addition to becoming a two-way communication vehicle, this approach also provides practical solutions to many problems, and it meets the ideal organization principle of having decisions (and actions) made at the level within the company closest to the problem.

Some companies require each supervisor to submit a copy of any objectives established during the meeting. Their fulfillment then becomes one of the supervisor's objectives—objectives on which the supervisor's performance is measured.

Meeting Guide

The structure of these meetings varies by company and survey results. Beginning on the next page is a supervisor's guide created by one company. It is provided as a base for developing your own approach and is also included on the accompanying disk for your use.

A Supervisor's Guide for an Employee Opinion Survey Feedback Session

Introduction

This Supervisor's Guide has been prepared to assist you in communicating the results of our employee opinion survey to the employees in your area of accountability. The guide is meant to be used in conjunction with training provided by the human resources department.

If you have any questions about the survey results or how to conduct the feedback session, be sure to check with the human resources department.

Preparations

In order to conduct this session you need to make the following preparations:

Obtain an adequate size room with tables and chairs. The table arrangement should be a conference or U-shaped table. There needs to be adequate number of seats for all employees.

Have paper and pencil for all employees or require each employee to bring paper and pencil.

Obtain a flip chart with appropriate markers.

Obtain an overhead projector.

Obtain transparencies of the dimensional survey pages for your department. Also, obtain transparencies for any other elements of the survey results to be communicated to the employees.

Review with your department vice president her responses to the survey results for her area.

Obtain from the department vice president any specific overall action plans that have been made as a result of the survey.

Obtain correct factual information for any issues raised by the survey.

Review the survey results for your area of accountability and identify areas you feel should be discussed.

Notify employees of the meeting time and location. Generally, a meeting of this type requires between two and three hours.

Session Outline

Open the session and describe the meeting	15 minutes
Review survey results	60 minutes
Develop action plans	60 minutes
Conclude the session	15 minutes

Session Guide

Arrive ahead of time to ensure that the room is properly set up and all materials are present. When the employees arrive, be sure they all know each other. Make introductions if necessary.

When all employees are there, or it is the scheduled starting time, whichever comes first, begin the meeting.

Opening the Session (15 Minutes)

Good morning/afternoon. Today we are here to review the results of our employee opinion survey. More specifically, we are going to be looking at the results for our area of accountability. That is something new with this year's survey. This is the first survey in which we have been able to examine the results for units smaller than the entire company.

After I review the results with you, we are going to spend some time deciding what actions we can take to help further improve conditions of being an employee of our company. In total we will probably be here three hours. It is an important three hours. It is an opportunity for us to examine our perceptions and to take the type of actions for which we have been empowered.

Now, are there any questions?

Answer any procedural questions before continuing. However, specific questions about the survey results will probably be answered during the session. If questions arise any time during the session that will not be answered in the session, you may want to record them on a chart pad and post it at the side of the room. Then following the meeting, answers can be obtained for these questions and communicated to the employees.

You might want to have the department vice president open the session. Before you examine your area's results, the person to whom you report may want to comment on the overall departmental results. However, it is best that the departmental vice presidents not stay for meetings conducted by people reporting to them.

Survey Results (60 Minutes)

The statistical results are reported as graphs. Each graph includes the results for a specific item or dimension by:

Total company

Your department

Be sure to check your survey results and know exactly what groups are reported. If an overall communication to all the employees has already been published, refer to it briefly. On the other hand, the company may want you to distribute some type of overall communication booklet at this meeting.

The statistical survey reports are presented in sections:

Demographics—the number of people in each reported group

Dimension—results by dimension—major employment area

Levels of significance

Item—results by specific question

Ranking of questions by number of positive responses

The relationship of importance and satisfaction for the dimensions and benefits.

In addition to the statistical results, 110 employees provided written comments. You need to check with the person to whom you report to determine if there are written comments appropriate and available for your department. Also, an analysis was prepared and delivered by the company's consultant and is available for review. It can provide insights into overall company results.

All graphs are reported by the percentages of positive, neutral, and negative responses. Generally, surveys of this type are analyzed by their positive responses, but we have found it more useful to view all three categories of responses.

The majority of questions on the survey (161 in total out of 163) had five possible responses. For individual items the five responses are shown. Also shown are variations from the overall total by groups and their levels of significance.

Levels of significance refer to the statistical evidence that any difference is a real difference and not just due to chance. Levels of significance on this survey are calculated two ways. A single asterisk indicates that there is a statistically significant difference between the number of a group's positive responses and that of the total employees. A double asterisk means it is even more significant. Differences without asterisks are not considered significant.

The statistical report includes a table of level of significance by dimension and group within the report.

The demographics indicate the number of people who identified themselves as being within a certain group. Keep in mind that sometimes people purposely or mistakenly identify themselves as in the wrong group. In any event, you should compare the number of people in your area of accountability who participated in the survey and the number who claimed to be in that area.

Reviewing the responses to 163 questions can be somewhat mind-boggling. Most people do best if the dimensions serve as the basis for the review. Dimensions are collections of responses for related questions.

Once dimensions have been reviewed, then any particular item in which your area of accountability differs significantly or any particular item which you feel your area of accountability should handle should be discussed. The negative items should only be reviewed if they make a contribution to understanding the survey.

As you show each dimension transparency, you might want to read the analysis of the overall company results and the company's response. Then, communicate your reaction for the overall department.

Go slowly. Give the employees time to understand each chart. Reveal only one chart at a time. Answer questions when they are asked.

Developing Action Plans (60 Minutes)

When you have completed reviewing the survey data, you should move into action planning. Actually, this is the key point of what you are doing.

First, communicate any action plans the company has already made as a result of this survey. Next, communicate any action plans for your department that have already been made. Then, you want to identify areas that require action plans. You might want to list these and then have the employees respond. On the other hand, it might be more effective to get their responses first and then list any additional ones you have.

Once the areas for needed action are identified, you need to develop specific action plans. The best way of doing this is to divide the employees into subgroups. Depending on the number of areas, assign each subgroup one or two plans and have them develop specific actions. Then, reconvene the entire group, have each subgroup present its results, and discuss whether or not to add to those plans.

The final outcome of this discussion should be a list of action plans by area. Each action plan should have a due date and some type of measure of successful completion. Also, accountability for accomplishing the action plan should be assigned.

This should be a very positive part of the meeting. It is empowering to involve employees in improving their area and two-way communication between you and them.

One thing you want to avoid is any defensiveness. Even if employees are wrong, their perception is their reality. You need to talk things through. Don't defend. If necessary, provide factual information and try to discover if the facts someone believes are wrong. Do not argue. In this session you are a leader more than anything else.

Closing the Session (15 Minutes)

When the action plans are prepared, you need to close the session. Do so on a positive note. You may want to have your department vice president attend to hear the action plans and have him provide some recognition to the group for their effort.

The action plans from the group should be written and distributed to the group and your vice president.

Conclusion

This chapter has dealt with the process of reporting results of the employee opinion survey to employees through the employees' supervisors. This approach allows for two-way communication, and recalls from the Introduction of this book that two-way communication is seen as the most effective way to utilize employee surveys.

In the next chapter, a series of checklists is provided to assist you in reviewing the book and implementing the process.

CHAPTER 17

SURVEY CHECKLISTS

When all is said and done, a company, its chief executive, and ... (the) whole management team are judged by one criterion alone—performance.

HAROLD GENEEN AND ALVIN MOSCOW,

Managing

This chapter contains summary checklists for all the steps described in this book for the development and implementation of the recommended employee opinion survey format. They are provided as a quick and convenient method to review the steps as you are implementing them.

Development Steps for Implementing an Employee Opinion Survey

Select a survey format.

Establish a specific objective for the survey.

Identify the purposes for which survey information will be used.

Identify the employee population to survey.

Identify the conditions of employment and their subareas to survey.

Determine where and when to survey.

Determine the employee demographics to identify and report.

Select the types of questions and responses.

Develop the questions for each area.

Sequence the questions.

Develop a security system.

Prepare the survey documents.

Prepare the survey administration rules and instructions.

Select the survey administrators.

Describe the tabulation report format.

Schedule the survey.

Notify the employees.

Train the administrators.

Obtain supplies and equipment.

Administer the survey.

Analyze the initial tabulation.

Obtain additional required information.

Prepare a management report.

Prepare a final report to employees.

Deliver the final report to employees.

Prepare individual supervisor reports.

Train the supervisors in a survey report meeting method.

Conduct supervisor-led survey report meetings.

Select a Survey Format

Written

Group-administered

Mailed

Individually administered on site

Online

On-site, computer-administered

Available on any computer

Focus group

Interview

Combination of two or more formats

Questions to Ask in Deciding Which Format to Use

What are the reasons for which you are conducting the survey?

How many employees do you have to survey?

How much time will your survey require to complete?

Which format best fits the culture of your company and abilities of your employees?

What is the employee survey history at your company?

A Recommended Format

A written survey administered to groups of employees or an online self-administered survey

Follow-up focus groups and/or interviews to obtain any required additional information

A survey report that includes:

❏ Analysis of all conditions of employment
❏ Satisfaction and importance perceptions for each condition of employment
❏ Comparisons with past survey results
❏ Management reactions and plans for each condition of employment

Use of survey results in two-way communication

Development of objectives based on survey results

Employee Opinion Survey Guidelines

Do not conduct an employee opinion survey without a clear and specific objective.

Obtain management support for a complete survey plan before beginning development.

Be sure you have fully and in a timely fashion communicated the objective of the survey and use of its results to all employees.

Make provisions to protect employee confidentiality.

Administer the survey objectively.

Deliver survey results as promised.

Do not attempt to affect survey results.

Do not use employee opinion surveys for voting.

Establish a Specific Objective for the Survey

A good objective is one that is based on a specific reason for the survey and describes its primary goal, for example: to discover employee perceptions regarding their satisfaction with conditions of employment.

State your objective in one sentence beginning with the word "To" and ensure it answers the questions:

❐ Why do you want to conduct an employee opinion survey?

❐ What are the areas for which you want to know employees' opinions?

❐ What employees do you want to survey?

Identify the Purposes for Which Survey Information Will Be Used

State each in one sentence beginning with the word "To."

Write them in descending order of importance, that is, write the most important purpose first, the next most important second, and so on.

If you have more than eight purposes listed, review them to determine:

❐ Is each too detailed, limited, or specific?

❐ Is it possible to combine two or more?

❐ Are all really important?

Examples

To identify areas requiring management attention

To identify changes in employee perceptions from previous surveys

To communicate to employees their collective degree of satisfaction with all conditions of employment

To discover employees' satisfaction along with their perceptions of the importance of working conditions

Identify the Employee Population to Survey

Identify the total group and any subgroups of employees to survey.

Determine the number needed from each group.

Select the number of employees required from each group.

Use random sampling if fewer than all employees selected.

Sample Size Determination

Consider the degree of confidence you require.

Consider the maximum allowable error you will accept.

Consider variations in the employee population.

Random Selection Techniques

Assign numbers:

❏   Assign each employee in the population a number.

❏   Use consecutive numbers.

❏   Use a table of random numbers to select by number.

Draw names:

❏   Write each employee's name on a separate piece of paper.

❏   Mix the names.

❏   Draw the number of names required.

Use systemized selection:

❏   Obtain a list of employees.

❏   Select in a systemized fashion—every so many names.

Initial Communication to All Employees

Communicate to Management First

The objective of the survey

> When it will be conducted

> That results will be reported to all employees

Who to ask questions

Who may be requested to assist

When employees will be notified

Use media normally used to communicate to management

Communicate to All Employees

The objective of the survey

> When it will be conducted

> That results will be reported to all employees

Ask questions of your supervisor

Who may be requested to assist

Use media normally used to communicate to all employees

Identify the Conditions of Employment and Their Subareas to Survey

Develop a starting list based on:

- ❐ Internal questionnaires and meetings
- ❐ Previous surveys
- ❐ This book's list
- ❐ Consultants or consulting firms
- ❐ Published surveys
- ❐ Employee handbooks

❏ Company policies and procedures

❏ A questionnaire

Develop your typical conditions of employment—survey dimensions:

❏ *Immediate Supervision*—the direction, planning, and control exercised by the individual to whom you report

❏ *Job Assignment*—the responsibilities and authorities of the job you are asked to perform

❏ *Communications*—the communications you receive and provide

❏ *Performance Measurement*—the evaluation of your individual job performance

❏ *Compensation*—the cash rewards you receive for your work

❏ *Benefits*—the noncash rewards you receive for your work

❏ *Security*—the confidence you have in your safety and continuation of employment

❏ *Executive Management*—the leadership, planning, and control exercised by the senior executives of the company

❏ *Equal Treatment*—the fair and nondiscriminatory treatment you and other employees receive

❏ *Training*—the training provided for your current job, changes to your job, and future jobs

❏ *Career Opportunities*—the opportunities to increase your accountability and grow within the company

❏ *Facilities*—the environment in which you work and the availability of necessary equipment and supplies

❏ *Overall Company*—all the things that contribute to the company and its operations

Identify dimension subareas:

❏ Specific elements of each

❏ Elements currently requiring questions

Determine Where and When to Survey

Consider required completion date.

Consider the time to complete survey.

Consider the dates of previous surveys.

Consider the dates that will be appropriate in future years.

Consider holidays, busy times, and vacations.

Consider events that may be planned.

Consider when most employees are available.

Consider the requirements of other locations.

Consider union contractual requirements.

Consider legal and contractual requirements.

Determine the Employee Demographics to Identify and Report

Typical Demographic Groupings
Typical Employee Classifications

- ❏ Executive
- ❏ Management
- ❏ Supervisor
- ❏ Administrative and clerical
- ❏ Sales
- ❏ Professional
- ❏ Hourly
- ❏ Temporary
- ❏ Permanent
- ❏ Full-time
- ❏ Part-time

Department

❏ Group departments of a few employees with similar departments.

❏ Use numbers or titles employees know.

Length of Service

❏ Use ranges.

❏ Recognize anniversaries that affect conditions of employment:

1. Retirement
2. Vacation
3. Vesting
4. Assignment

Race:

❏ Use correct terminology.

Gender

Age:

❏ Use ranges.

Location—if employees are from more than one location.

Other Possible Demographic Groupings

Education

Marital status

Length of department service

Length of service in current position

Length of time it should take to complete a survey

Select the Types of Questions and Responses

Question Types
Objective

Multiple-choice

Essay

Fill-in

Response Types
Scale

    ❑ Odd or even points

    ❑ Number of scale points

Answer Sheets
Machine-tabulated

Written responses

Number of Possible Questions
Calculate the total survey time.

Calculate the number of essay questions.

Calculate the number of demographic questions.

Calculate the time for the introduction and instructions.

Calculate the number of dimensions.

Calculate the number of subareas to survey.

Develop the Questions for Each Area

Consider the type and number of questions for each dimension.

Consider the type and number of questions for each subarea.

Consider supplemental questions.

Consider the tabulation methodology.

Sequence the Questions

Group by dimension or mix.

Group by dimension and then by type.

Group by type and mix.

Group by type and then by dimension.

Group by importance.

Order of Types of Questions

Importance scale

Agreement scale

Amount scale

Rating scale

Satisfaction scale

Multiple-choice

Fill-in

Essay

Develop a Security System

Group- and Individually Administered Written Surveys

Distribute cards with demographic information for admittance.

Check off attendees from master list.

Mailed Surveys

Have one survey mailed to each employee.

Have one return envelope mailed to each employee.

Do not accept reproduced surveys.

Establish last postmark date for acceptance.

Online Surveys

Program controls.

Use randomly selected passwords or numbers.

Interviews and Focus Group Meetings

Assign employees.

Consider not giving employee names to interviewers and meeting leaders.

Prepare the Survey Documents

Survey Question Document

Introduction

❏ Purpose (objective) of the survey
❏ Reporting of survey results
❏ Use of survey results
❏ Confidentiality of survey responses

Answer Sheet Document

Machine-scored

❏ Ensure enough response categories for the number of questions.
❏ Ensure the correct number of responses per question.
❏ Include some form of identification space.
❏ Include practice question responses.
❏ Have response numbers agree with question numbers.

Written questions

❏ Have some form of identification space.

❒ State questions.

❒ Have space for responses.

Prepare the Survey Administration Rules and Instructions

Group- and Individually Administered Written Surveys
Rules

❒ There is no talking among participants.

❒ If participant must leave the room, he must leave all survey materials at his chair.

❒ Participants may take as long as necessary to complete the survey.

❒ There is no time limit.

❒ If only a part of the survey is completed, only that part will be tabulated.

Instructions

❒ Include how to respond to the survey questions.

❒ Include instructions on using codes or passwords.

❒ Show how to cross-identify answer sheets.

❒ Include submission procedures.

Mailed Surveys
Rules

❒ Only employees can complete the surveys.

❒ Reproduced surveys will not be accepted.

❒ Surveys are to be returned in provided envelopes.

❒ Include the date of latest accepted postmark for surveys.

❐ Participants may take as long as necessary to complete the survey.

❐ There is no time limit.

❐ If only a part of the survey is completed, only that part will be tabulated.

Instructions

❐ Include how to respond to the survey questions.

❐ Include instructions on using codes or passwords.

❐ Show how to cross-identify answer sheets.

❐ Include submission procedures.

Online Surveys
Rules

❐ Only employees complete surveys.

❐ Include the date of latest accepted survey.

❐ Participants may take as long as necessary to complete the survey.

❐ There is no time limit.

❐ If only a part of the survey is completed, only that part will be tabulated.

❐ If a participant must leave the computer, she must log off and log back on later.

❐ Only one log-off/log-on is allowed.

Instructions

❐ Include how to respond to the survey questions.

❐ Include instructions on using codes or passwords.

❐ Show how to cross-identify answer sheets.

❐ Include submission procedures.

Select the Survey Administrators

Sources
>Internal
>
>External
>
>Combination

Considerations
>Time available
>
>Abilities
>
>Number required
>
>Availability
>
>Credibility
>
>Cost

Describe the Tabulation Report Format

Considerations
>Populations of employees by total participants and demographics
>
>Question responses by dimensions and subareas
>
>Full reports by requested demographics
>
>Written responses by departments
>
>Any requested correlations
>
>Any requested comparisons
>
>Any requested comments or analysis

Schedule the Survey

Group- and Individually Administered Written Surveys

Obtain facilities.

Obtain surveys.

Obtain answer sheets.

Obtain supplies.

Obtain equipment.

Allow time for make-ups.

Mailed Surveys

Obtain prestamped addressed envelopes.

Obtain instruction letters.

Obtain surveys.

Obtain answer sheets.

Have outgoing envelopes addressed.

Prepare packages for mailing.

Allow time for make-ups.

Online Surveys

Have surveys programmed.

Obtain equipment.

Obtain security.

Allow time for make-ups.

Notify the Employees

Initial Communication

Communicate to management first:

❐ The objective of the survey

❐ When it will be conducted

❏ When results will be reported to all employees

❏ Whom they may contact with questions

❏ Who may be requested to assist

❏ When employees will be notified

❏ Use of media normally used to communicate to management

Communicate to all employees:

❏ The objective of the survey

Final Communication

Is conducted a week or two prior to survey date

Uses normal communication media

States objectives and purposes

States survey dates

Includes format and procedure

Lists make-up procedures

Lists location(s) of survey

Includes individual employees scheduled by supervisor

Includes information on reporting of survey results

Recommends seeing supervisors with questions

Train the Administrators

Subjects

The company's objective in conducting the survey

The confidentiality of survey information

The dates of any past surveys

Any particular problems associated with past surveys

The facility, equipment, and supplies required and arrangements for them

When and how survey feedback will be given to employees

Who is assigned and will be available to help with any questions or problems

The security procedures

Any employee assigned to an administrator for security assistance

The mechanics of the survey (forms, answer sheets, etc.)

The instructions

The name and telephone number of someone to call for assistance

The individual schedules

Checklist of Equipment and Supplies

Written surveys administered to groups:

- ❐ Location
- ❐ Pencils or other marking devices
- ❐ Pencil sharpener, if needed
- ❐ Enough surveys and answer sheets for all participants
- ❐ Envelopes and/or drop box

Written surveys administered individually at a single location:

- ❐ Private room or cubicle for completion
- ❐ Pencils or other marking devices
- ❐ Enough surveys and answer sheets for all participants
- ❐ Envelopes and/or drop box

Online surveys:

- ❐ Available computers
- ❐ Loaded and accessible survey
- ❐ Passwords or numbers

Obtain Supplies and Equipment

Written Surveys Administered to Groups

Confirmed location

Pencils or other marking devices

Pencil sharpener, if needed

Enough surveys and answer sheets for all participants

Envelopes and/or drop box

Written Surveys Administered Individually at a Single Location

Confirmed private room or cubicle for completion

Pencils or other marking devices

Enough surveys and answer sheets for all participants

Envelopes and/or drop box

Mailed Surveys

Cover letters

Enough surveys and answer sheets for all participants

Addressed and stamped return envelopes

Addressed outgoing envelopes

Online Surveys

Confirmed available computers

Loaded and accessible surveys

Passwords or numbers available

Administer the Survey

Written Surveys Administered to Groups

Ensure location is available.

Ensure administrator is at location.

Ensure all supplies are at location.

Ensure envelopes and/or drop box is at location.

Ensure participation security at location.

Written Surveys Administered Individually at a Single Location

Ensure private room or cubicle is available.

Ensure administrator is at location.

Ensure all supplies are at location.

Ensure envelopes and/or drop box is at location.

Ensure participation security at location.

Mailed Surveys

Ensure all are mailed.

Online Surveys

Confirm available computers.

Ensure surveys are loaded and accessible.

Ensure passwords or numbers are available.

Make-Ups

Contact any employee missing scheduled survey participation.

Contact any employee not returning mailed survey by due date.

Contact any employee not completing online survey by completion date.

Analyze the Initial Tabulation

Review Received Tabulations

Response intensity:

- ❑ High negative responses
- ❑ High neutral responses
- ❑ Equal positive, neutral, and negative responses

Importance and satisfaction:

- ❐ High importance and high satisfaction
- ❐ High importance and low satisfaction
- ❐ Low importance and low satisfaction
- ❐ Low importance and high satisfaction

Correlations:

- ❐ Conflicting responses
- ❐ Inconsistent responses
- ❐ Levels of significance
- ❐ Relationship of dimension responses to overall company results

Changes from prior surveys

Differences with any external surveys

Written comments that refer to unidentified factors

Tabulators' comments

Obtain Additional Required Information

Identify Any Additional Information Required

Describe information.

Identify source.

Select procedure:

- ❐ Questionnaire
- ❐ Focus group
- ❐ Interview

Determine number to contact.

Conduct questionnaires, follow-up interviews, and/or focus groups.

Prepare a Management Report

Use tabulated results and additional information acquired.

Structure of Report

Description of survey format

Description of survey procedure

Description of dimensions and subareas

Number and types of questions

Demographics of respondents

Graphs or tables of each dimension question by:

❑ All employees

❑ Major demographic groupings

Commentary on dimension reports

Graphs or tables for all subarea questions by:

❑ All employees

❑ Major demographic groupings

Commentary of individual subarea questions

Comparison with previous survey results or external surveys

Relationship of dimension satisfaction responses to importance responses

Written comments

Commentary on written comments

Summary of overall results

Plan for communicating results to employees

Executive summary

Delivery

As printed document

At group meeting

Obtain

Management's reactions

Management's action plans

Structure for report to employees

Method for report to employees

Prepare a Final Report to Employees

Structure

Description of survey

Survey objective and purpose

Description of survey dimensions

Commentary on each dimension:

❐ Summary of responses

❐ Comparison with past surveys

❐ Comparison with external surveys

❐ Brief analysis

❐ Management's reactions

❐ Management's action plans

Overall summary

Description of next steps

Department meetings

Deliver the Final Report to Employees

Employee meeting:

❑ Survey results given by person accountable for conducting survey

❑ Management's reactions and action plans given by senior manager

❑ Department meetings described by human resources representative

Booklet

Employee newsletter

E-mail

Computer

Prepare Individual Supervisor Reports

Survey reports by individual departments

Train the Supervisors in a Survey Report Meeting Method

Review and discussion of overall survey results

Review and discussion of individual department results

Review and discussion of department meeting agenda and approach

Practice in conducting department meeting

Delivery of department survey results to each supervisor

Conduct Supervisor-Led Survey Report Meetings

Overview of survey results for the company

Questions and discussion of overall survey results

Review of survey results that apply to the department

Questions and discussion of department results

Identification of areas of needed improvement that can be addressed at the department level

Establishment of objectives for improvement based on survey results

Assignment of accountability for implementing objectives

Establishment of a follow-up meeting to review progress in fulfilling objectives

INDEX

ABOUT THE AUTHOR

John H. McConnell is president of McConnell-Simmons and Company, Inc., a management consulting firm located in Morristown, New Jersey. The firm specializes in human resources products and services. Prior to establishing his current company in 1974, McConnell held a number of human resources executive positions with Capital Holding; M and M/Mars; Garan, Inc.; and Wolverine Tube Division of Calumet and Hecla. He has undergraduate and graduate degrees from Wayne State University in Detroit, Michigan. He has written more than two dozen books on management and human resources, including *Auditing Your Human Resources Department* and *How to Identify Your Organization's Training Needs*, and has been a frequent speaker at AMA seminars, the AMA Management Course, and national and international human resources conventions.